MW00711913

For Thomas Lux

Editors
　　　Travis Denton & Katie Chaple

Layout & Design
　　　Travis Denton

Special Thanks to
　　　Poetry@TECH,
the School of Literature, Media and Communication
and Georgia Tech's Ivan Allen College

terminus is published with generous support from

Poetry@TECH
www.poetry.gatech.edu

terminus seeks to publish the most thought-provoking, socially and culturally aware writing available. While we aim to push the boundaries of general aesthetics and standards, we also want to publish writing that is accessible to a wide audience. We seek to live up to the highest standards in publishing, always growing and reaching new levels of understanding and awareness both within our immediate community and within the greater communities of our country and world. *terminus* accepts unsolicited submissions year-round, but keep in mind that most of our content is solicited. We encourage simultaneous submissions, so long as we are notified. Address all correspondence to: ***terminusmagazine@gmail.com***.

a Poetry@TECH
sponsored publication

terminus is printed by Lightning Source and distributed by Ingram.

copyright 2017 by *terminus magazine*
no part of this publication can be reproduced without the express
written consent of *terminus magazine* and its representatives

ISBN: 978-0-9961-5-6

The *terminus* logo was designed by Natalie Farr

Front & back covers, inside cover, and excerpt on page 8
by Brian Hibbard

Front Cover: *Dog on Ball 38*, 36 x 36.
Inside Cover: *Having a Ball 10*, 48 x 36.
Back Cover: *Having a Ball 34*, 36 x 48.

We recommend you check out more
of Brian Hibbard's work online at
www.hibbardfinearts.com

Contents

Featuring
Poetry@TECH's 2017-18 Visiting Poets

Art

Poetry

NonFiction

Fiction

Georgia Tech's
School of Literature,
Media, and
Communication presents

Georgia Tech | **Ivan Allen College** of Liberal Arts

www.poetry.gatech.edu

poetry
@ Tech

mcever poetry reading
with

February 22, 2018
location
Kress Auditorium   **7:30 p.m.**

Aimee Nezhukumatathil

the sixteenth annual Margaret T. and Henry C. Bourne poetry reading
featuring

September 28, 2017
location
Kress Auditorium   **7:30 p.m.**

Christopher Collins

Bruce McEver

Tyehimba Jess

Vijay Seshadri

Billy Collins

a spring poetry event
featuring

April 12, 2018
location
Kress Auditorium   **7:30 p.m.**

Victoria Chang

an evening of poetry
featuring

November 2, 2017
location
Kress Auditorium **7:30 p.m.**

Stuart Dischell

Anis Mojgani

Matt Hart

David Bottoms

Tarfia Faizullah

McEver Chair in Poetry

Travis Wayne Denton

2017-18 Visiting McEver Chairs

McEver Chair in Community Outreach

Visiting McEver Chair

Katie Chaple

David Bottoms

THE KRESS AUDITORIUM
Renewable Bioproducts
Institute at Georgia Tech
500 Tenth Street, NW
Atlanta, GA 30332

All events are free and open to the public.
No tickets or reservations are required.
A book sale and signing to follow all readings.

The Kress Auditorium Parking:
Plenty of free parking available just in front
of the building's entrance or through the
gate, which is straight ahead as you turn off
10th Street.
For more directions & parking info visit:
www.ipst.gatech.edu/amp/

For more information about
Free Poetry Workshops in
the community go to
www.poetry.gatech.edu/poetry_class.html

Laure-Anne Bosselaar

Lux

from Latin *lux* (light)

That rain. All day no light & that rain.
It trails me to work, through streets & traffic,
weeps against windshields & windows.
What is it that shadows me so?

It trails me to work, through streets & traffic,
clings to me, insists, *He's gone*—
what is it that shadows me so?
This rush of rain (a contstant *shush*)

clings to me, insists: *He's gone*—
He's gone. And you, so far away.
This rush of rain (a constant *shush*)
wanes before I can make sense of it.

He's gone. And you, so far away.
In the steel sky, just now, a scythe of light
wanes before I can make sense of it:
that light a shiver in every drop.

In the steel sky, just now, a scythe of light
weeps against windshields and windows,
that light a shiver in every drop.
That rain. All day no light & that rain.

Acrostic DeLux

Triple-syllable-word zapper, article-

Hexer, Red Socks fan. Book-

Ogre, skeet shooter, word

Monger, metaphor man.

Ar-ti-cul-la-tor, bat-

Swinger, Crane

Lover, huge heart. Here's to that ticker

Up Clock Street, here's to his

Xanthous locks.

Laure-Anne Bosselaar is the author of The Hour Between Dog and Wolf, Small Gods of Grief, *winner of the Isabella Gardner Prize, and of* A New Hunger, *selected as a Notable Book by the American Library Association. The editor of four anthologies, and the recipient of a Pushcart Prize, she teaches at the Solstice Low Residency MFA Program at Pine Manor College. Her next book* These Many Rooms *will be published by Four Way Books in early 2019. She lives and teaches in Santa Barbara, CA.*

Billy Collins

Just Looking

I'm trying to figure out what the cat
is looking at from her spot
on a window seat in a bit of morning sunlight.

As far as I can see,
there's nothing going on outside
except the vibrating shadows of trees

and the swaying of the wind chimes,
yet she remains stock-still,
unblinking, with her ears pricked up.

But wait, there's the mailman
and a little later, a kid bicycling by,
and those white clouds in the distance—

now that they have my attention—
could be the thought balloons of earth
that might tell us something

about what Mother Nature is thinking,
if only we could read them,
and if that really is her name.

And that's when I noticed
the cat had turned away
and was heading toward her bowls in the kitchen,

where I followed her
and made myself a grilled cheese
and tomato sandwich on whole-wheat toast

and then returned to my study
where many projects awaited me
and where she was nowhere to be seen.

Empty House

I wonder—
did she happen
to play something new
on the piano

before she left

or was it just the breeze
from the door
she left open
that turned the page?

Going for a Walk as the Drugs Kicked In

It's Friday, the sun's all over everything
after a long week of constant rain.
The clouds have moved on
to hover over other roofs.
The irises are showing their white faces
streaked with yellow and purple.
The bees are out again
making thousands of visitations.
The beaver swims with a stick in his mouth.
The otter is looking out his window.
The butterfly doesn't seem to know where it's going.
Ample and worthy is the air around me.
I am only able to take in one bird at a time.
A fruit tree has started to sing.
The little town is farther away than ever.
I have my arm around the otter,
holding him by the shoulder.
The scene out his window is so plentiful
and everything is billowing with our love.

Billy Collins has published ten collections of poetry, including Questions About Angels, The Art of Drowning, Sailing Alone Around the Room: New & Selected Poems, Nine Horses, The Trouble With Poetry and Other Poems, Ballistics, Horoscopes for the Dead *and* Picnic, Lightning. *His most recent book of poetry is titled* The Rain in Portugal *(October 2016) and is a* New York Times *bestseller. In June 2001, Billy Collins was appointed United States Poet Laureate 2001-2003. In January 2004, he was named New York State Poet Laureate 2004-06. He is a former Distinguished Professor of English at Lehman College of the City University of New York. In 2016 he was elected a member of the American Academy of Arts & Letters.*

Denise Duhamel & Julie Marie Wade
A Collaboration
from *50 States*

Indiana

My friend Bob was dying in Indiana. He had lived his whole life, all eighty-four years, in South Bend—a devout atheist in a town of equally devout Catholics. The drive from Louisville takes five hours. The road lolls like a tongue, long and flat inside a mouth of endless trees. We sat by the window in Bob's storybook house, watching robins and cardinals hop nimbly from branch to branch, debating which poem I should read at his funeral. He was so calm about death, always matter-of-fact, saying "I like the one with the *Goddamn* in it. Promise you'll ruffle some feathers for me." I promised. I drove back for the memorial, held in an art gallery instead of a church. I breathed *Goddamn* into the microphone, and half the audience gasped. One man, perhaps agnostic, suggested I should join the local chapter of Toastmasters. "We'd love to have you," he grinned. In his will, Bob left me his orange couch and two matching footstools. Beneath the pristine cushion a cream tag with gold calligraphy read *Made Especially for Pletcher's Village Furniture Shop, Highway 6, Nappanee, IND*. My third trek to South Bend was for the couch. We rented a Uhaul at a Texaco station. My beloved drove our car home, and I followed in the cab of a huge metal box, only a couch and two footstools rattling around inside. It was then I cried, all the trees around me stripped and dying. *"Goddamn you,* Indiana. *Goddamn."*

Nebraska

What they don't tell you about the Cornhusker State is that the wind there doesn't blow—it *howls*. Like, say you were driving late into the night, due east from Wyoming to Missouri. Say you were taking Interstate 80 because you wanted the beaten path, were afraid to deviate in a place that got Brandon Teena killed, his tombstone flipped around to "Teena Brandon," that family horror called saving face. Say you had heard good things about Lincoln and Omaha, were banking on a nice college breakfast in a safe college town. Say you had even seen *About Schmidt* earlier that year and liked it, grafting your own lives onto an Alexander Payne film. Weren't you, after all, "quirky with heart," worthy of an RV road trip, a more-than-cameo from Kathy Bates. Now say it was well over ninety degrees, and the air-conditioner in the car had begun to wheeze. Say you were looking to catch some shut-eye, just for a couple of hours. Say a bridge had washed out near Sidney, and all the motels were full. You could see the No Vacancy signs flashing red as the devil's eyes for miles. And say when you rolled down the windows and let your fingers dangle in the humid air, you began to hear it—a child wailing, a woman weeping, a desperate man pleading with the moon to turn him lupine at last. In two heartbeats, you were heading south on 76 toward Colorado.

New Mexico

In Taos I marveled at the turquoise and skulls as well as the skulls deco-
rated with turquoise. I was in my twenties and couldn't afford much then.
I was just happy to see Georgia O'Keefe colors and drink booze. I'm not
even sure how I afforded the alcohol exactly. There was a good liquor
store in Taos full of dusty bottles and day workers. Always something on
sale—and I wasn't that fussy. Taos was brimming with artisans and art-
ists, tacos and sparkling rings. Though turquoise is technically a semipre-
cious stone, that summer I thought it as beautiful as any diamond. Maybe
when I got married, I told myself, I'd ask for a turquoise ring and wear a
gown the color of turquoise. But who was I kidding. I'd never get mar-
ried if I kept drinking. How could I keep my secret with a partner who
might wake up in the middle of the night and see me chugging vodka? *So
what*, I'd tell myself, *marriage is for losers. Marriage is for provincial losers, right?* I
asked the bejeweled steer skulls, their antlers varnished and painted black.
I stood in front of the tourist traps, trying to see my reflection in plate
glass windows, trying to line up my eyes to the missing eyes of each skull.
When a steer's spirit said to me *you better quit the spirits, kid*, I blinked and
started to run. *Fuck death*, I thought, *fuck that know-it-all skull*. I went back
to New York, but that steer followed me to each medicine cabinet mirror.
Now I say, *New Mexico, thank you.*

Oklahoma

When I saw the tumbleweed, I knew I couldn't live there, even though
I was offered a terrific job. Even though there were startup funds and
travel funds and houses cost so much less than where I currently lived.
When I saw all the beautiful windmills twirling their arms, I almost
changed my mind. When I found out the windmills were a front for
T. Boone Pickens, the tumbleweed rolled over my third eye again.
Get a group of artists together talking about real estate, and soon one
of them will say, "Hey, we should start a commune where the land is
cheap." Claudia Emerson and I had the idea of buying an old motel
and living there with other older poets and artists in our dotage, but
then she died quite young. Oklahoma would be a great place for a
commune/old age home, but try to get a group to uproot all at once,
and you'll see how impossible the task. I wouldn't have made a good
pioneer, though I wish I'd seen *Oklahoma* on Broadway. Square-dancing
cowboys and farm girls are more interesting to me knowing there is
a pretzel vendor and subway right outside. When I didn't take the job
I felt like a snob, a city slicker taking the hiring committee for a ride.
But part of me truly wanted an adventure, a do-over in a place I never
expected I'd be. I imagined myself finally belonging to the land, feeding
my free-range chickens from a pocket in my apron, then twirling like a
windmill singing "O-K-L-A-H-O-M-A."

Vermont

I taught a summer workshop for high school writers at Bennington College, where the art teacher had an aneurysm and died in front of her students. The teacher was in her thirties, maybe younger, and the program director had to call her parents who came to get the body and collect her belongings. I was starting to feel my own mortality in terms of nausea and a sharp pain in my back, which was wrongly diagnosed at the local ER as a kidney stone. The high school teachers were living in a dorm, and I had to bring my sieve down the hall whenever I peed to catch the rock the doctor thought was growing inside me. It turned out I did indeed have stones—gall, not kidney—and at the end of that summer, I had an operation at St. Vincent's in New York City that left a scar across my abdomen. Bennington is beautiful, lush and green in July with an adorable downtown and a Ben & Jerry's. Just down the road, in Burlington, are the corporate offices where I learned that no white-collar employee could make more than seven times that of the lowest paid employee. This made me want to support the ice cream, which couldn't have been good for my gallbladder. Vermont is idyllic in so many ways, but because I didn't have health insurance that summer, all I remember is worrying that I could die young like that poor art teacher. We'd met the first day at orientation. Though she was not yet a friend, we had planned to go to the discount designer outlets on our day off.

West Virginia

Don Knotts, famous for his role as Fife on *The Andy Griffith Show*, was born in Morgantown, WV, where a star boasting his name on the sidewalk appears in front of the New Metropolitan Theater. Though I'd watched the 1960s sitcom, my father was the one who laughed at all the jokes. I was a fan of Don Knotts because of his portrayal of Mr. Limpet, a secret agent who becomes a fish to destroy a Nazi submarine. I didn't know much about World War II when I first saw *The Incredible Mr. Limpet*, but I understood fairytale romance and Mr. Limpet's love of Ladyfish. Don Knotts stares into an aquarium singing "I Wish I Were a Fish," and later becomes a cartoon bottom-dweller who still wears Henry Limpet's signature glasses. I happened to be upon this sidewalk on the 50th anniversary of *The Andy Griffith Show*, Morgantown a hub-bub of activity. A local reporter put a microphone in front of me and asked, "So what was your favorite episode?" I faltered, telling her the story of Mr. Limpet, how I wanted to change myself into an animated fish after I saw it. She had never seen the movie and didn't seem to understand what I was talking about, yet there I was on the 6 o'clock news. I watched myself and started to cry, missing my father, who was no longer breathing air or water, who had been dead one year.

Denise Duhamel and Julie Marie Wade have published collaborative essays in Arts & Letters, Bellingham Review, Cincinnati Review, Connotation Press, Green Mountains Review, Nimrod, No Tokens, Passages North, poemmemoirstory, Quarter After Eight, The St. Ann's Review, *and* StoryQuarterly. *Their first collaborative book* The Unrhymables *will be published in 2018 by Wild Patience Books. They both teach in the MFA program at Florida International University in Miami.*

Victoria Chang

Dear P.

Your thoughts come out as frays as howls
they are like the bubbles from a fish's mouth
that rise and disappear globules of letters in
a liquid envelope today a woman's voice
sounds old wood thick deep the voice is
mine it takes deeper cover against the sky
against its blue shin that never answers with
anything but clouds and rain my voice digs
with its fingers in the wrong direction dead
down it goes head down my throat drags me
one day I will bang and bang on the soil from
below but you and your briefcase will not hear
me one day you will look down at the manhole
pass through my breath rising up as steam

Once Barbie Chang Worked

Once Barbie Chang worked on a
    street named Wall

once she sprinkled her yard with
    timed water once

she wore lanyards in large rooms
    all of the chairs

pointed in the direction of one
    speaker and a podium

once she stood up at the end to
    leave but everyone

else stood up and began putting
    their hands together

and that started her always wanting
    something better

A Little City Resides

A little city resides in Barbie Chang's
        hand as she handed

her life down to her children the little
        city wasn't worth much

slum mulch made it unlivable but she
        loved the lights at night

her hand filled with stars animals stared
        at the glow the lights made

sense to them once a woman named
        Millicent asked Barbie if

her diamonique necklace was real if
        the city in her hand was

real Barbie Chang had built an entire
        world based on the

corner of an eye out of a thousand split
        second views only then

did she realize her world was all sky
        she had forgotten

the land Millicent was from Connecticut
        and told Barbie Chang

she was the favorite at the firm she
always asked her which

partner she was working with why
she parted her hair

down the middle always asked her
where she was from

Barbie Chang wished she had a father
named Don Swan

then she would know how to respond
swimming in a

pond twenty years later it rains and
from below the

woman's words still beat onto her
body like snow

Victoria Chang's fourth book of poems, Barbie Chang, *is forthcoming from Copper Canyon Press. The Boss (McSweeney's) won the PEN Center USA Literary Award and a California Book Award. Other books are* Salvinia Molesta *and* Circle. *She was awarded a 2017 Guggenheim Fellowship. She lives in Southern California and teaches at Chapman University and the Orange County School of the Arts. You can find her at www.victoriachangpoet.com.*

Stuart Dischell

Inside the Weather

Who punished the wind that lost control?
Who lashed the rain for joining in?
Who scolded the air for aiding them?
Or the sky for its dominion?
Who made the clouds permissible
To havoc in the ranting storm?

Dark trees sway in the yard.
Everything is. Nothing is like.
Branches fall in the universe.
Stars die in the night.
Telescopes are useless
To know the movements of neighbors.

And the Emperor in his chamber
Thunders bring me fruit on a plate.

Nothing about Dogs

A yellow one and a silver one, both as shaggy
As a sixties bathroom carpet and toilet seat cover,
Sleep under the awning of the porch in a place
They have learned is out of the rain. The yellow one
Looks dirtier because it is lighter but the silver one
Is larger and smells worse, I am told, by a woman
Who appears out of nowhere in her driveway
(Nowhere being outside my field of concentration),
And says the yellow one is on its last legs,
And as if to prove it, it stands on trembling forelegs,
Before flopping down once again on its pal
Like old-time bums in a doorway.
The dust should rise, but the rain tamps it down.
She tells me, her neighbor, their owner,
Has been locked up in the state hospital
For the insane and she looks after them
In case he ever gets out. I recall the story
In the paper. A naked man in his yard fired
A rifle at the sky, but nothing written about dogs.

Sonnet with Paint in Its Hair

The day's work looked flawless,
The whole kitchen spackled,
Primed, and coated, and still
Time to cook my supper.
Then I saw them on the sill
Above the sink, the spiders
In the paint, the twin beans
Of their bodies covered and
The whiskers of their sixteen legs
Caught in hints under the layers.
Like lovers they were, like lovers
Stuck in the lava of Vesuvius.
(Darling reader, if you exist,
Please forgive the excess of my metaphors.)

Attic and Basement

When she said I had no room
For her in my life, all I saw when I closed
The phone was emptiness stretched out
Like the earth beneath my house,

And unlike her body those words never
Left me, like snow affixed to the roof
Of the world I had forgotten while
Living as I do so close to the ground.

Stuart Dischell was born in Atlantic City, NJ. He is the author of Good Hope Road, *a National Poetry Series Selection,* Evenings & Avenues, Dig Safe, Backwards Days *and* Children With Enemies *and the pamphlets* Animate Earth *and* Touch Monkey, *along with the chapbook* Standing on Z. *His poems have appeared in* The Atlantic, Agni, The New Republic, Slate, Kenyon Review, Ploughshares, *and anthologies including* Essential Poems, Hammer and Blaze, Pushcart Prize, *and Garrison Keillor's* Good Poems. *A recipient of awards from the NEA, the North Carolina Arts Council, and the John Simon Guggenheim Foundation, he teaches in the MFA Program in Creative Writing at the University of North Carolina Greensboro.*

Jacqueline Duffy

Why is there something rather than nothing?

"…the super-ultimate why question…"
Why Does the World Exist?: An Existential Detective Story
—Jim Holt

A question for any context:
feeling or lack,
abundance or absence.
His book interrogates philosophers,
scientists, religious for the why of it,
the origins' unfolding being settled.
The history of hypotheses, stories,
places for god when he's left to the gaps
makes metaphysics—myth.

Fourteen billion years ago energy unspun
its singularity. Matter, space, time began,
continue to expand in the vacuum
two-thirds dark energy and dark matter.
Who knew we were so empty?
(We have such expectations.)

We cannot ask before matter else we
meet our ends in our beginnings.
That alpha and omega conundrum.
But parallel worlds exist,
in theory. They impinge and here
and there bubble up, an infinite
regression, deferring the question,
us now, right here, my body
moving over yours, thinking.

It's just that I expected a different conversation

not of you watching *Wheel of Fortune*,
but this morning sun returns to my window.
From my desk the magnolia may be close enough to jump to,
its rain-polished green cards collected, sewn
into a wreath to mark my door from all the places
bits of information stream towards. Those bytes
risking the pull, like fascinated moths, milling aimless, near
the lamp-lit window—are black-holed by ring-wraithed
intelligence and lose all direction. Our magnetic fields
lap and cohere, as signals bend the warp and weft,
but wheels are spoked not woven, so they turn
to the fixed places they turn to. Fortunes,
sun, and honey dripping my upturned breasts—
all the turnings of all the worlds and all—
like the jewels in Indra's knotted web reflect
every possible existing, every path on the wheel,
the dharma of the cosmological constant being,
the impetus for longing.

Coupled stray capacitance

*"Stray capacitance…is unwanted in a circuit [and] can result in a
disruption of normal current flow."*
—*Learning About Electronics*

My heart's desire is a book called: *Higher Voltage—
Resistance Makes the Toaster Hot*
like the river's capacity to rise
but not the reversible lane out to get me
(opposing traffic slaloming upwards)
not distortion, not impedance, but ground
and balancing the chakras' circuit,
Ohm's compassionate furnishings
there in the fundament
humming along in proportion.
White light crown to root to crown,
settling down in the furnaced room.

*Jacqueline Duffey lives in Marietta, GA. Having completed her MS in Counseling, she is currently looking
for work in the field. In an earlier life, she got a creative writing MFA from Alabama.*

Bethany Maile

How Lady Antebellum Wrecked Country Music (in Eight Movements)

1 A (countrified) introduction

I order a whiskey seven and press it to my neck. My hair sticks to my forehead, my fingers swell; I am a puddle. I wear linen shorts and a loose-tank top, but the heat is so thick I feel swaddled in the gauzy cotton. It is August in Tucson, and the bar's patio is packed with aspiring writers, all students in the University of Arizona Master of Fine Arts program. Tomorrow classes begin, but tonight is meant for introductions.

Despite the 100+ temperature, I wear cowboy boots. They stick to my legs, but they are worth the discomfort. I love these boots. Love the way they point at the toe, the way they give me an extra two inches, the way they clack brightly on pavement. And when people ask where I am from, I say *Idaho*, and they say *nice boots*, and I say *you bet*.

I grew up in Idaho, and I realize, as I walk onto the patio—crowded with Eastern transplants, New Yorkers and Bostonians who have come west for the first time—that I look a little like a prototype. I wear cowboy boots, crank Tammy Wynette from my truck's staticky speakers. But my indulgence in being this type of Westerner is not totally deliberate. It happened slowly, organically. I married a man with a pickup who loves John Prine and Conway Twitty. I learned I preferred the way my legs look in El Gringos. That I liked ordering a whiskey even more than

I liked drinking it (like the boots, the drink feels tough, unexpected from a woman, and this unexpectedness is a quick thrill). So I wear my boots and drive my pickup and play Loretta Lynn for anybody who'll listen.

Two weeks into the school year, in a chicken-fry-drive-in called Wishbone, I eat with a graphic memoirist from Connecticut. With a French fry fixed between her fingers, she points up and listens.

"Isn't this like Garth Brooks or something?"

I listen. The song is a sorrowful, smooth ballad; a man and woman do vocal gymnastics around each other. A piano plinks along in the background. Though there's a mild twang in the singers' words, the song is more Celine Dion than Brooks.

"Not even close," I say.

"But this is the kind of thing you like, right? It seems very *Idaho*."

The single is catchy, sure. The singers belt out the chorus, each vowel a slow, countrified drip. But the song drowns in over-production, layers of guitar, auto-tuning. And I bristle at the suggestion that this is *Idaho*. In what way, I want to ask? The man whines "I need you now" one last time, and the woman whispers vocal flourishes, and the piano closes us out. I want to tell her this song is crap, cheesy and over-the-top. I want to tell her it doesn't seem very *Idaho* to me.

The song is called "Need You Now," and after that first encounter in the chicken shop, I hear it everywhere—in line at the bank, seeping from someone's car at a red light. And then I see the singers for the first time. Glowing from the television screen sits a woman with Farrah Fawcett hair and fist-sized bangle earrings. On her right, a short, brunette man slouches away from the camera; on her left, a long, blonde man squints to the screen—a too-cool recognition of his televised audience.

The week before the 52nd Grammy Awards, Chris Harrison (most widely known as the shoulder-to-cry-on host of ABC's dating show *The Bachelor*) sat down with Lady Antebellum. The group had just released their sophomore album, received a slew of Grammy nominations, and was preparing to perform at the event. A year earlier, the Grammy folks knighted Lady Antebellum "Best New Country Artist/Group" for the band's self-titled debut album. It had been a fame-studded year for the nascent group.

The trio perched on barstools while a green screen of the LA valley flickered behind them. After lauding the group's year of accomplishments, Harrison asked, "I don't mean to make you nervous, but what do you bring to that show this year? Because it's not just country. It's everybody in that room." The musicians paused. Mr. Harrison's question bordered on rude: *This isn't just the Country Music Awards. It's the Grammys. The big time. Can you handle it?* The three members of Lady Antebellum, front man Charles Kelley, backup singer Dave Haywood, and front lady Hillary Scott, each shiny with eyeliner and pomade, nodded kindly as Mr. Harrison asked if they could bring it. Then, speaking for the trio, Kelley responded, "We're just excited to [...] represent country."

2   The birth of a Lady (first as I've imagined it—mired in hardship—and then as it more likely occurred)

It seems a notable parallel that just as I presented myself as a prideful Idahoan, Lady Antebellum exploded on the music scene. Surrounded by those MFA, East-coast-transplants, I found the group's drawling familiar in the warmest way. But for all that familiarity, I remember how I recoiled when my friend said the group seemed so *Idaho*. So what I'm most fascinated by, then, is my distaste for the band. I dislike the single (so sappy and over-produced), and I am surprised that I am not charmed by the group's overt countryness. They are, by their own definition, country representatives. It seems I should find solidarity in this.

At first glance, the band's formation sounds like something from a country western biopic, like *Coal Miner's Daughter* or *Walk the Line*. A story of just-arrived dreamers banking on luck, a story of tough shakes. I imagine it this way: long, blonde Chris Kelly packed a guitar and a pair of boots and lit out for Nashville. Once there, he sang on street corners and bars, his only compensation a free basket of fries at the end of the night—just another cowboy alone on the stage. His money thinning, he called his buddy, Dave. The two stockpiled ballads and boot-scoots and kept playing the Nashville circuit, hoping to break through, like Montgomery Gentry or Brooks and Dunn. But, as is so often the case, the pair went unnoticed.

Enter Hillary Scott. A Nashville native, Scott's parents were country singers. She knew the industry inside out, and she'd been singing since she could crawl. Mostly though, she changed the chemical compounds of the group from a familiar male duo to a universally lust-inducing mixed-sex trio. With male *and* female lead singers, listeners could hear the estranged lovers sing *to* each other (in the way of Johnny Cash and June Carter, Tammy Wynette and George Jones). Or, in perkier numbers, flirtation and banter could ensue. Hillary Scott brought a complexity and sexuality that would serve the band well.

In truth, what Scott brought the group, more than anything, were connections (reference her industry-mired parents), and even this isn't the whole truth. That season of Kelley and Haywood playing for spare quarters on street corners? Unlikely. Kelley came to Nashville in 2006, just three years after his older brother, Josh Kelley, rolled into town. Josh, who is a mildly popular pop singer, gained most of his celebrity for marrying the busty, doctor-playing actress Katherine Heigl. All this to say Kelley (Charles) came to town connected. Six months after arriving in Nashville (which is enough time to rent a pad and have a few meetings with your semi-successful brother's people), he'd found Scott on MySpace, talked his childhood buddy into coming down to Nash-Town, and had successfully put together Lady Antebellum. Within the year the group was signed to Capitol Records, along with Katy Perry, LCD Sound System, and, once upon a time, the Beatles.

2a Another note (concession? confession?) on band formation

So Lady Antebellum came to Nashville connected. Big deal. Good for them. They didn't have to wait it out and suffer like so many singers. But what gives me pause is this: from the beginning, Lady A seems to have been a precisely planned, carefully

So Lady Antebellum came to Nashville connected. Big deal. Good for them. They didn't have to wait it out and suffer like so many singers.

packaged product, something molded into an alluring object cranked out of the Industry Machine. And maybe that's fine. Certainly it's happened before. But in country music, fans (I?) have always expected a certain hard-knocks history, a certain paying of dues. I think of Cash selling appliances by day and playing bar-gigs at night, and how he came to Sun Records and asked to sing gospel-inspired songs, and everyone told him *nobody'd buy that*, but he kept on keeping on till somebody would. I want country artists who rose to the top by their own volition, folks who pressed on in the face of adversity.

3 Regarding the aforementioned album, *Need You Now* (a section which should be read by those deeply interested in the troubles associated with genre straddling or in the failings of genre straddling as a comment on inauthenticity)

After the promise of the band's first album, the sophomore record, *Need You Now*, catapulted Lady Antebellum to major mainstream success. Not everybody gets to play the Grammys, after all. The album squatted at number one on the *Billboard Hot 100*, and three of the singles nabbed the same top spot. Four weeks after the album's release, it was certified platinum, and the *LA Times* called it "impressively well considered." They continued, "Lady A delivers an emotional punch." In the world of country pop, the group was riding high.

Not everyone was impressed, though. *The Washington Post* agreed the album's title track packs some emotional sting and that Scott's vocals are pure honey, but went on to say, "The sad-drunk swirl rendered so acutely [in "Need You Now"] quickly gives way to mush on the disc's 10 remaining tracks, a cluster of soft-rock tunes that boast just enough steel guitar to keep Lady Antebellum CDs in the country music aisles."

The Washington Post touches on a fundamental dilemma of country pop music. The label seems like a misnomer, country *pop*.[1] Each artist that has tried to straddle genre boundaries has, at some point, heard this criticism. Kenny Rogers, one of the first country pop artists, la-

---

[1]   Really, though, isn't the broader term *country western* problematic, too? With most C & W artists hailing from the southern states and with few songs mooning over Western territory, the genre might better be termed just *country* or *country southern*.

mented, "For country music, I'm not country enough. Everywhere else, I'm too country." So the balancing act is tricky, I'm the first to admit.

After the Harris interview, with the group cast in the unhealthy tint of a television's glow and promising Grammy success, I listen to the album online. Though I cannot palate it, the ubiquitous single does all the things successful pop music should. Heavy harmonies plague the chorus, Scott's vocals are crystal clean (if not reminiscent of Kelly Clarkson's or, at other times, Alison Krauss') and the chemistry between her and co-lead singer Kelley pulses through at every turn. Most important, the number's catchy. The song opens with synthesizer and slow piano, then electric guitar rises to the front, and they are rolling. But spare a few inordinately long vowels and the mention of a shot of whiskey, nothing about this track feels particularly country.[2]

When Lady A isn't struggling to straddle the country/pop border, it borrows from more successful pop-rock numbers. In "Stars Tonight" the band offers a Guitar Hero version of an AC/DC song. Lead guitar kicks off with a percussive, distorted staccato, and it's clear that nobody's strumming here; no, these strings are gettin' wailed on. The sound is forceful,

When Lady A isn't struggling to strad- dle the country/ pop border, it bor- rows from more successful pop- rock numbers.

abrupt, and hard rock all around. It's a tidier, less raw AC/DC, but a rock-n-roll nod none-the-less. Halfway through the number, the pounding guitar mellows, and where I was reminded of Angus Young, I now think of Bryan Adams, and the "Summer of '69" intro flits through the chorus. In the background, vocalists yell *hey, hey* and I can only imagine them to be fist-pumping.

Toward the end of the album, though, things perk up. Right out of the gate, "Something 'Bout A Woman" is startlingly country. The song begins with dobro, then leads right into acoustic guitar, bass, and piano, and when Kelley lights in, he is drawling his heart out. For once he sounds more like George Strait than Rob Thomas. It is, by a long ways, the album's most successful track (though interestingly never released as a single, as far as I can tell).

---

2   Or as my friend might say, *Idaho.*

In the album-closer, the group is back to half-hearted country tunes masquerading as pop songs. In "Ready To Love Again," Scott takes over (and really, with pipes like hers why hasn't she sung more leads?), and while the singing is pleasant enough, the song itself reminds me of something I would have loved about ten years ago, after my first break up, which occurred in gym class while I wore too-snug mesh shorts and the whole class looked on; the event prompted me to spend weeks locked in my bedroom sulking in a bean bag listening to songs just like "Ready To Love Again."

My complaints with the album aren't just that it isn't country enough. Put plainly, it isn't good enough. The appeal of country pop is not lost on me. I have seen Tim McGraw in concert more than once, and each time I have flushed at his low drawl and snug jeans. Brooks, McGraw, Strait, they are all crossover stars, and I appreciate their music deeply. But they also don't blow quite as intensely as Lady Antebellum.

And here, perhaps, is why. The balancing act is difficult. As *The Washington Post* pointed out, there is only enough steel guitar on *Need You Now* to (barely) keep Lady Antebellum on country airwaves. And when Lady A isn't doing the country thing, they aren't being original (even that golden nugget, "Need You Now" is a straight rip off of the Alan Parsons' Project's "Eye in the Sky"). Maybe that's the real trouble. It's one thing to push into pop territory; it's another to rip off pop classics, only to blend them with warbled vocals and the occasional bluegrass rhythm. While borrowing from other artists is nothing new in the pop world, audiences expect that the new interpretation at least be well done.

Really, though, what I'm asking for is authenticity. I want to listen to a Lady A track and sense they wrote this song *inspired*. That these aren't just old classics repackaged, and that the group isn't a carefully combined product, orchestrated by a pop singer's manager. I want to know that if they'd come to Nashville unconnected and had to hock blenders Cash-style until they got a record deal, they would have. I want to know that they combine country and pop because they believe there is some chemistry that can be unlocked between the two, or that they feel like they somehow embody both genres, or that they've thought about these combinations at all.

4 A description of what Lady A looks like live

Despite my objections to the band's latest album, when a girl from class offered me tickets to their Phoenix show (She'd planned on taking her boyfriend who was visiting from New York. She'd figured a country band would be an appropriately Arizona-type thing to do, but he was sick, and I liked this sort of thing, right?), I took them.

Lady A plays to a three-thousand-seat arena, and the place is packed. Packed with nineteen-year-old girls in cheek-revealing jean skirts, mall-bought straw hats, pleather cowgirl boots, tags freshly snipped. They come in costume. Plaid dresses abound. But no one sports the real deal Western garb: Wrangler's or square-toed Justins. Instead, two-hundred-dollar skinny jeans are tucked into pleather boots.[3] This is a standard sensation at every Western event. When attending a rodeo, businessmen wear pearl-snaps for the first time; soccer moms pull on pink modeling boots. So, too, at country music concerts, attendees don cowboy hats and jean jackets. Though Lady Antebellum's country styling is subdued at best, they remain country enough to prompt this kind of rural imitation.

While the audience comes bedecked in its Western finest, Lady A eschews the boot heels and belt buckles. Spotlights swirl. Strobes flash. The trio, hands clasped, waits out the crowd's roar. Kelley, a head taller than anyone else, wears boots, but the Italian zip-up variety. Steven Tyler jeans and a tuxedo blazer. His hair tousled in the pseudo-reckless way of teen heartthrobs. Haywood sports skinny jeans, a sweater vest, and a fedora; he is an Urban Outfitters poster boy. Between them, head still cast down,

---

3   And I wear red ankle boots, purchased at a boutique in NYC's SoHo district. I wear them regularly, and chose them coincidentally, with zero intention of tapping into the Western-ness of Lady A, but perhaps this only underscores my larger devotion to Western costuming. Maybe that I wear this type of get-up on a daily basis makes me even more culpable; I assert my affection for country charm always, not just in the company of country pop megastars.

her leg shaking to the beat, poses Hillary Scott. Like her bandmates, she wears black pegged jeans. A tunic of blue sequins catches the strobes' light. Her hair has been blown out to Victoria's-Secret-model volume, and she balances pointy-toed in a massive pair of sequined spike heels. The guitar licks through the intro to "I Run to You," a Grammy-nominated single from their debut album, and then the band breaks formation. Where Miley Cyrus would gyrate against a pole, or Madonna would claw the ground, they look up. For thirty seconds the crowd has waited for a hip shimmy or leg kick, some kind of motion, and with the fanfare of a dozing cubicle worker, they lift their heads. And that is all.[4] Then Kelley sings. Scott harmonizes. They turn and gaze at one another. Haywood strums his guitar, standing a little too close to the duet, the odd man out.

During fast numbers, each of them moves as if they are dancing. Kelley squats a little and stamps a foot and poses hard, his head tossed back to the light, the microphone tipped above him. Never once does he seem lost in the music. Never once does he seem to have forgotten that three thousand people are watching on. Each time he moves, it is with the forced posing of someone trying too hard.

And Scott isn't much better. She limps across the stage, confined to short, flat-footed steps in her massive heels. She waves one arm above her head always, and sometimes wiggles her knees a bit, but as soon as her hips engage the dancing becomes clumsy.

Haywood may dance. It is hard to tell. He is seldom in the spotlight.

Eventually, Kelley introduces the band, which is composed of an army of guitarists (mostly electric), keyboardists, bassists, and a drummer. Though he is from Georgia, there is no trace of an accent until he says, "Dave Haywood on the gee-tar." He introduces the other three guitarists and sticks with this pronunciation. Similarly, Scott, the Nashville native, offers no Southern accent, and I wonder about those hard Rs in their songs, how *heart* becomes a two-syllable word in these mouths. Whether or not Haywood has an accent remains inconclusive, as he never speaks.

After the introductions, red lights flood the stage, and the guitar percusses through the auditorium as the "Back in Black"-esque num-

4   Clarification: I am not asking Lady A to perform as something they're not, which would be another mode of inauthenticity, but I am asking that they not be boring. To wash a stage in red pulsing lights is to infuse an audience with a certain expectation, and it's on the performers to rise to that occasion.

ber, "Stars Tonight," blasts. As was expected, the trio pounds fists and stomps legs and makes like rockers, sort of. But the song, again, is too refined for real hard rockery. Beneath Kelley's quavering vocals and awkward dance moves, this attempt at rock-n-roll falls flaccid. Despite the red-washed stage and pounding guitar solo, there is no energy. The spotlight breaks on Kelley, and he twitches his hips a little and grips the mic stand and seems uncomfortable with the level of enthusiasm expected of him. He is incapable of delivering on such a charged song.

The whole show goes on this way. In fast numbers, the band members twist and kick around the stage, feigning enthusiasm, feigning rock edge. During ballads, Kelley and Scott embrace in the spotlight, Haywood strumming lonesomely beside them.

Halfway through the set, they hit their stride. The band unplugs. The pulsing lights die. All unsuccessful attempts at stage tricks vanish. The trio stands in the center, and an accordionist, upright bassist, dobro player, and mandolin player form a horseshoe around them. "Something 'Bout a Girl," their one unabashedly country number, fires up, and the players stand on an unsmoking stage, without roaming spotlights, and they play the song. Plain as pie. Scott and Kelley stand poised, planted, singing into the audience, not at one another. Haywood plays with the other musicians. The song, unsullied with pop ambitions, is good. Kelley and Scott, freed of any obligation to entertain as a pop artist might, forget about forced dance moves and center stage poses. They move loosely, naturally, and by the end of the song, the audience is quiet for a moment, lulled, believing.

5 A word on why Lady A doesn't just cut the country and go pop (or cut the pop and go country, whichever your inner-music critic prefers)

That the most successful number (by my estimations) is the band's one true country song begs the question: why isn't Lady Antebellum a Clearly, Lady A does not dazzle like most pop artists. Pop fans want flaming stages, smoking cages, dresses made of ribeyes.

country western band? Clearly, Lady A does not dazzle like most pop artists. Pop fans want flaming stages, smoking cages, dresses made of ribeyes. And if there is no spectacle, they want dancing. Trapeze! Cirque-de-Soleil acrobatics! Make it worth the $50 bucks! Lady Antebellum cannot do this. And what they lack in pop star antics, they do not make up in looks. Nobody in the group has the soap star attractiveness of most pop singers. While these demands for beauty are illogical and misplaced (pure bull shit, really), they are, regrettably, a fundamental tenet of pop success (especially these days, when a singer's mug is everywhere—blogs, MTV, YouTube). The reality is, Lady A ain't pretty enough for pop. They can't dance or entertain well enough for pop. In the world of pop, Lady A can't cut it.

> There is not a cowboy boot or hat on stage. The men use eyeliner, wax their eyebrows, pomade their hair. Kelley introduces Scott as the "woman with the best heels in all of country."

More than anything, Lady Antebellum's music and performance suffer from a split-identity. Recall the Chris Harrison interview when Kelley was "just proud to represent country." Yet every decision the band has made (musically, sartorially) is decidedly un-country. There is not a cowboy boot or hat on stage. The men use eyeliner, wax their eyebrows, pomade their hair. Kelley introduces Scott as the "woman with the best heels in all of country." And she flashes her sequined pumps and says, "They're Miu Miu, and I love them." Musically, the group is more influenced ("influenced" being the kindest word for Lady A's relationship with classic rock numbers) by rock acts than country artists. As they clomp around the stage and fist-pump in the red light, it is clear that Lady Antebellum has tried, more than anything, to be as un-country as possible.

While it's evident that the band could not function as a mere pop act, I cannot blame them for trying to pass in the pop world. Country pop sells. As a recurrent attendee of both country pop and country western concerts, I can attest to the financial prowess of country pop. I have seen C & W's largest acts—John Prine, Lyle Lovett, Loretta Lynn, Emmylou Harris. These folks need a stool and a stage, a fiddle and a guitar. No pulsing lights and steam machines. But, comparatively, no one attends these shows. Prine plays in small theaters; I've seen Lyle Lovett four times and never once in a three-thousand-seat auditorium. The money is in the pop world.

6 The part where we consider why this matters

But perhaps Lady Antebellum's motives are less business-like. Maybe they are inspired artists, and maybe country pop feels truest to them. It's significant that the genre emerged in the mid-20th century, just as housing tracts spread with newfound speed through the American West, as farms morphed to tract house mazes. The country western way of living has become endangered, and the West I know, if it were to borrow the music world's verbiage, is country pop. Consider my hometown. The majority of Idahoans live in the Treasure Valley, a land of strip malls and barn stalls; one-ton pickups parked in three-car garages; cowboy hats purchased for the sole purpose of attending rodeos or concerts. So if music is a reflection of culture, then of course country pop has outmatched country western. Pure western—musically, culturally—hardly exists in this country.

And Lady A offers an honest representation of where we are and where we're headed, as opposed to most pure country western artists who are so often fixated with where we've come from. The group tells the story of *now*. Mercantiles flipped for strip malls; housing tracts abutting cornfields; dirt roads paved and made wider; a trio of Nashville singers making like KISS with black leather and stage makeup and seizure-inducing lights (but throwing in the occasional long-voweled drawl); a confused mish-mash of rural and rock.

7 A (probably unfair) comparison

Admittedly, I am most satisfied with country music when it dwells on the West's past, when it gives in to the dominant mythology of this place—bucking broncs and tough people and long dusks purpling the prairie. I think of Lyle Lovett, whose lyrics are unwaveringly country. He sings about cornrows and biscuits and ten-gallon hats. And while these may be common components of Lovett's world, my experience with them is limited. I have never punched cattle through a river; I have never polished a gun; I have never blown a tire just south of Reno. But I put on a Lovett album and tell myself this is an authentic Western experience, that it adheres to my pre-established notions of this place, to the (admittedly false) idea that this is a land of bulrush marshes and dust-spangled breezes, a place where every season's summer.

Not surprisingly, at the lyric level, Lady Antebellum rarely seems country. Save the rare mention of white churches and barefoot women and whiskey, the group sings about breaking up and moving on and growing up. Unlike Lovett's, Lady Antebellum's lyrics reflect experiences I've actually had. There is nothing idealized about them. I know Lady A's world. It is vague and therefore universal. Who hasn't wanted to drunk-dial an ex? Or wade in self-pity after a breakup? People get dumped. They get bummed out. They make regrettable booty calls to exes. Perhaps then, Lady A's lyrics are inherently honest, undeniably true.

7a a word on authenticity, by way of definition

My affection for Lyle Lovett reveals much about my insistence on authenticity. Thus far, I have charged that Lady A suffers from inauthenticity (the bad pop rip-offs, the phony stage presence, the problematically split country-pop identity). But in many ways, Lady A is nothing but authentic. The stories they tell are universal, and therefore relatable; they describe experiences I've actually had, and here I recall John Berger who said in his book *Keeping a Rendezvous*, "Authenticity comes from a single faithfulness: that to the ambiguity of experience."

So I should clarify. Lady Antebellum inauthentically represents my preconceived (and faulty) image of this place (a myth). And so if Lady A is meant to authentically reflect a myth, then they fail. And in this way, Lyle Lovett succeeds. He absolutely embodies the myth of this place—all his six-shooters and longhorns and honey-lit plains.[5] But if being authen-

So I should clarify. Lady Antebellum inauthentically represents my preconceived (and faulty) image of this place (a myth). And so if Lady A is meant to authentically reflect a myth, then they fail.

---

5   I suspect Lovett realizes he's offering us a dream, that he knows there is very little "real experience" in his lyrics. For evidence, see the song "In My Own Mind." The

tic means being true to the reality of experience, then can one have an authentic myth? It is like asking for the true version of a lie. A myth is, at its core, a fiction, a story people have told themselves. And so my demand for an unflagging commitment to the myth, for an authentic portrayal of something that doesn't exist, is oxymoronic at best. I realize this.

8 Why 7a doesn't matter

Admittedly, country western artists sing about a culture that no longer exists (or, perhaps, that never existed). Friday nights spent boot-scootin' or fishing under the stars are idyllic, mythologized, of course. And Lady A doesn't go there. They don't offer this dishonest portrayal. Maybe this deserves credit.

But I am reluctant to offer them this. That Lady A sings about experiences I've had doesn't matter, because maybe in country music, these rules don't apply. Maybe here reality loses bearing. Maybe I come to music—to country music especially—for a story, not for the actual. I come to gain entry to an unknowable world. I come to access something I know is bygone. I have said that Lady A represents where we are right now, this minute; they embody the West's transition from a distinct rural culture to the homogeny of suburbia. They are all about the *now*, the immediate (and consider their lyrics: the fleeting experiences of this very second—booze binges, drunk dials, etc.). And while Lady A thrives in the current moment, Lovett points to where we've come from. He's fixated with the past (even the Texan cattle rancher knows the place he longs for now exists only in his mind), and in his lonesome cowboys and tough women, I see an elegy to a world that's disappeared.

Here I see not the dangers of romance (which so often keeps us nostalgic, prone to the most potent delusions) but the power. In Lovett's romance, he is spurred to elegize, and the very act of elegizing recognizes a thing as dead, as gone, as worthy only of memory. So I come (romantically, knowingly) for the dream of lilac breezes and boot-grooved porches. I come to pin down the vanished. I come for the memory. I come to mourn.

---

number (one of his few singles that didn't crack the charts, which I fear might have to do with its honesty) tells the story of a man who lives in a world where he plants in the spring, picks in the summer, hunts and fishes in the afternoon, and drinks coffee with his baby in dawn's warmest light. It's a landscape doused in sunshine, where only the best harvest rains fall, a place that exists—as the chorus and title tell us—only in his mind.

For all my disapproval, I must acknowledge that Lady A and I are not without our commonalities. I think of my friend at the chicken shack, mid-chew, freezing at the sound of the single, assuming this is something I know, something I like. *It seems very Idaho.* Or my classmate gifting me with tickets—*You like this sort of thing, right?* Lady A and I are both proud, on some level, to represent (be?) country. But I'm not sure either of us fully understands what that means.

I have said that the group poses too hard in the shadow of a thing it just isn't, and here I see the lamest reflections of myself. I wear cowboy boots to shopping malls and movie theaters. I drive my pickup to coffee shops. I have laid out my costume, if you will, as evidence of my (earnest) Idaho-ness, and while I genuinely like these things, nothing about them is authentic. I don't haul trailers or hay with my pickup; it could just as easily be a convertible. I could wear sandals or heels more purposefully than my boots. I have taken the functionality of the old world and reduced it to a stylistic flourish, like a whiskey-shot lyric or fiddle riff.

Like Lady A, I am a product of the New West, a blend of rural and suburban, Old West and New. I haven't thought twice about my boots. I like them, so I wear them. And maybe Lady A has been just as thoughtless yet earnest with its flashes of country. Maybe, then, some grace is in order.

Like Lady A, I am a product of the New West, a blend of rural and suburban, Old West and New. I haven't thought twice about my boots. I like them, so I wear them.

Lady A and I both identify ourselves, on some level, as "Western representatives," and I concede a certain bond here. To their credit, Lady Antebellum is a picture of the evolution from the Old West to New, the musical analog to the West's hybrid culture. They don't offer the dishonest (nostalgic, sentimental, mythic?) vision of wildrye meadows and burned-out cowboys. They've evolved out of that story. But their evolution, with its rock posturing and traces of old myth, is pretty shitty. They haven't totally quit this dominant narrative. They rely on it loosely. They drawl here and there. They throw in the occasional fiddle riff. They sport that Confederacy-esque group name.

But instead of being full-on romantic about it, instead of elegizing an old story of skipped rocks and young love acted out in the confines of a cornfield, they love it half-heartedly. They rely on it in the thinnest, emptiest way (a yeehaw here, a banjo there), and they fuse it with the bland vagaries of *now*. They fail to honor an old story in the way Lovett does, but they also fail to make our current moment meaningful or memorable. Instead, they merely bemoan the trivial inconveniences of the current. After all, people sober up, they get over break-ups, their drunken voice-mails are deleted. The experiences/problems detailed in Lady A songs are fleeting ones, quickly forgotten, easily recovered from; unlike Lovett who is haunted by something—a dream, a story, a place—that won't be so easily forgotten. One must choose the romance of *then* or the immediacy (genericism?) of *now*, and Lady A fails to pick a side (their lyrics say *now*, but their styling half-heartedly says *then*). They cannot have it both ways.

After eighty minutes of air-guitarring around stage, Scott and Kelley retake their initial pose—legs widespread, heads cast down, hands clasped; they have come full circle. Haywood ditches the guitar and takes to the piano. After the first four notes, the audience recognizes the melody to "Need You Now" and loses it. Kelley and Scott are unflappable. Heads down, they wait. The guitar cues, and seconds before her part, Scott lifts her head. With the melodrama of a Meatloaf video, she walks to the stage's end. Offering all the sexy-face she can muster—lips pursed, eyes slit—she moans the first line. At his cue, Kelley wades from the shadows, his free hand rubbing his chest and stomach as though getting through this intro is both painful and a turn-on. They pose. They belt harmonies. They ogle in the way of estranged lovers. They finish. The audience goes apeshit. They scream and whoop and stomp and clap. Scott blows kisses; Kelley waves for too long; Haywood flashes his palm once and is offstage. They disappear. The lights die.

The audience pounds, yells, begs for more.

Lady A retakes the stage, and I keep watching. For all I can't abide (the forced dancing, the hyper-produced singles, the half-hearted Western representation), I understand the group's confusion, their split-identity. In them, I see a bit of myself, clinging to the bits of the Old West I love—cowboy boots and country fiddles and Patsy Cline's sad songs. But while

And so I have seen all I can take. Three more minutes of Kelley and Scott singing rock-rip-offs as though the microphone is a hairbrush and they are pantslessly wailing in front of a bedroom mirror is more than I can bear.

we both sport vestiges of the Old West, I can't help but see a lack of affection in Lady A. They show no reverence or sincerity in their relationship to "country." And so I have seen all I can take. Three more minutes of Kelley and Scott singing rock-rip-offs as though the microphone is a hairbrush and they are pantslessly wailing in front of a bedroom mirror is more than I can bear. I shuffle my way down the aisle, past the wailing fans in glitter-rimmed cowgirl hats and unscuffed boots, and am turned out into the night. [6]

---

6   Though I left the concert dissatisfied, and Chris Harrison was leery of how well Lady A might deliver at the Grammys, it should be noted that the band took home the award for song of the year ("Need You Now"), best country album, best country performance, and best country song ("Need You Now" again). Taking home five Gramophones (a night-high), the Lady cleaned up.

Bethany Maile's essays have appeared in Prairie Schooner, River Teeth, The Normal School, High Desert Journal, Essay Daily, *among others. Her essay "Anything Will Be Easy After This" was a notable selection in* Best American Essays 2015, *and her piece "The Wild Ones" earned a Pushcart Prize nomination and a notable designation in* Best American NonRequired Reading 2012. *Her essay "We Sought But Couldn't Find" was included in* How We Speak To One Another: An Essay Daily Reader. *She lives in Boise, Idaho with her husband and two daughters.*

Chelsea Rathburn

On Domesticity

Around a blind corner, a shape in the road,
    dark and crouching, regards my car a half-

moment then sprints up the hill into the woods
    beside our house where my husband works inside.

It's not until it darts that I can name it,
    bobcat, that rumor that's haunted our neighborhood,

such as it is, for the last year, a specter
    picking off the groundhogs and feral cats.

I call Jim, breathless with what I've seen,
    and he rushes outside toward the danger,

which of course is gone. We are not mountain people—
    we do not hike or camp or commune with these woods

and how we came to live among others' second homes
    still baffles us—but these glimpses of the wild,

fleeting, vicarious, let us feel something
    more than our usual ennui, that vague

longing for the city and restaurants and lights
    that keeps us from feeling at home, and so we listen

for the clicks and howls of the unnamed in the dark,
    we look for the moving shadows beyond our lawn

perhaps because we know how much our own
        wildness has been tamed. I remember the fights

we used to have, how I'd collapse in tears,
        how gingerly we would touch each other

when we were ready to touch. And then we married
        and had a child, and there was no point to it,

to shaking the calm for the thrill of being right.
        What wild things are left are in our books:

Our daughter has us roar and shake our claws
        so she can say BE STILL! and silence us.

Introduction to Captivity

Green Thumb Nursery, Miami, Fla.

The days we wandered the drugstore aisles,
my cousin and I, counting out coins
for makeup we were too young to wear—
all of them gone, the drugstore too,
and the tropical nursery where
our parents dragged us despite the heat,
and the caged Capuchin who sat
scowling in that nursery. While
our parents wove through towering rows
of palms, we crouched beside the cage
to watch the monkey eat the grit
he pulled from his nose. We threw pebbles
into the cage and he ate them, too,
and reached for the pennies I flashed at him.
My cousin waved her lipstick next,
a purple only an eight year old
could love, and he scrambled for the tube.
Does a monkey smeared in Frosted Orchid
look that much worse than a child does?
At my cousin's wails, our parents came running
to find the monkey, lips aglow,
shaking a purpled fist in rage
or consolation through the bars.
Gone those lush and potted plants,
gone our burning girlhoods, yearning
to be older, to be prettier,
to be anyone else. It was lucky,
they told us, laughing, he didn't bite.

On Reading Maurice Sendak
Instead of Anaïs Nin

I wanted to write a poem about sex,
the sex of the long-married, about desire,
its departures and returns, by way of the bobcat
I met by chance on the curving lane below
our house—it bolted, I drove on. Its body,
the surprise of it—and my husband's body,
his muscular hide sleek as an animal's,
which after all this time should not surprise

but does. I tried to write the poem praising
my husband's form, the poem of gratitude,
joy even—I'll use that word—but a phrase
from a book intruded, a children's book, followed
by an actual child, our daughter dropping
her towel, shouting *Nay-Nay!* and darting away,
and it was her bright, joyful body I followed,
laughing, out of the poem and the room.

Introduction to Thanatology

On her seventh birthday, Alice said
we should try to make ourselves faint.
Her older brother had told her how:

you had to hold your breath while someone
pushed on your chest. When the first girl tried,
nothing happened, so I offered

myself up to their hands, Alice
giving orders at my feet.
On the count of three, I was no longer

at a slumber party but lying still
on a black table in a black room
with, yes, a slice of bright white light.

A stuttering sound, some fractured cry,
filled my ears in a voice that became
my own. And then the worried faces

as I came to, my mouth repeating
what I'd heard, what I thought was a word,
some urgent message from beyond

that no one understood. Alice
had been about to get her mother,
afraid they couldn't call me back

from wherever it was I'd gone,
but now she swore us all to secrecy.
We didn't know that kids could die

from games like this. We didn't know
that kids like us could die. We never
played again, but I remembered

sometimes how easy it was to slip
free of the body, like stepping from a robe,
and how certain I felt in that black space,

my friends and the darkness calling me.

Chelsea Rathburn is the author of A Raft of Grief *and* The Shifting Line, *as well as the forthcoming collection* Still Life with Mother and Knife. *Her poems have appeared in* Poetry, New England Review, Five Points, *and many other journals. A native of Miami, Florida, she now lives in the mountains of North Georgia, where she directs the creative writing program at Young Harris College.*

Dorin Schumacher

How She Won Him, 1910

—With Helen Gardner

I take a train to Brooklyn and knock on the door that says VITAGRAPH. The armpits of my dress are wet. A man in a bowler opens the door. "Helen Gardner, here to audition for the moving picture," I say. I put my hand out and he doesn't shake it. Two men are standing on a stage. A camera cranks in the background. A lady with frizzy hair leads me to a changing screen in a corner. I pull a shirtwaist and long skirt over my whalebone corset.

I can hardly breathe. But I want to be stylish. I want men to stare at me on the street. The corset makes my hips look even bigger.

"Stop," the director shouts. He tells a hand to replace the eight-foot backdrop with a painting of an office window.

"Sit on this chair. When the cameraman cranks, sit up straight, pound the typewriter, and look coy when your fiancé enters."

I learned how to look coy from my mother. I have a lot of practice.

He yells "Action!" I hit the keys. A young actor with a crumpled hat in his hands climbs the steps to the set. I smile and wiggle my bottom.

The Widow Visits Sprigtown, 1911

—With Helen Gardner

The wardrobe lady tucks my thick dark hair into a wig cap. She pulls on a curly golden wig.

They even want my irises to be blonde?

She slips a dress with padded breasts and hips onto me.

Not that I need any more flesh, but a little lift can always help.

I climb the steps to the stage that has a backdrop painted like a country town square, little storefronts, a theatre. The cameraman cranks the camera, his hand pulls the film at 16 frames per second.

Townies are waiting on the set. The young actors are paid to make eyes at me. I'm paid to wink back. The actresses have long faces. I glide across the set with a big smile.

I make up my own lines as I glide. Hello you country hicks I say. Don't you wish you could be sophisticated like me?

The camera stops.

The next scene is in a hotel bedroom but I'm not in it. The actresses find my wig and padded dress.

I wouldn't have gone anywhere without my wig and dress. Mistake in the story.

They throw the wig out the window. They light a fire in a can outside the door. The camera stops.

In my last scene, my fat and fifty boyfriend hears my screams, finds my wig on the ground, climbs a shaky ladder and throws it back into the room.

I hand him a snipped curl of the fake hair and a curl to each of the actors.

Good-bye you hicks.

The Show Girl, 1911

—With Helen Gardner, Maurice Costello and Florence Turner

The camera shoots from a wing of the stage. The dark-haired actress and three women dressed in flowing gowns twirl in a dance. A stagehand comes on stage and places a bouquet of flowers in the actress's hands. She turns her shoulder to the audience, acts startled, grabs a note from the flowers, turns again, kisses the note, and walks away from her floor marking. A dancer pulls her back.

I've never seen an incident like this in real life. No one would interrupt an actress in the middle of a performance to give her flowers and a note. If they did, she wouldn't take them. A critic attacked Vitagraph for producing a film with improbable, unnatural scenes.[1]

The set shows a dressing table and a mirror lined with lights. The actress sits at the table and admires herself in the mirror. A man in a tuxedo enters. She stands and smiles. He holds out a pearl necklace which she puts on. She swoons in his arms. He lays her down on a couch and exits. A dancer enters. Intertitle: YOUR ADMIRER IS MARRIED!

I wonder how she knows this because it's not in the scenario.

Outside a large house, the actress hides by the front steps. A sign on the house says DR. RENFREW, EYE SURGEON. A woman in a fur coat and two children climb the steps and go in the front door.

We don't know why the actress is at this house or who the woman and children are.
The actress sneaks in behind them.

She enters the doctor's operating room. A maid sits her in the patient chair and leaves. The actress turns the doctor's tools over in her hands. She lays the pearls on the stand beside the chair. Her admirer enters the room in a white coat. She speaks. He smiles a little and puts a cloth over her face.

He acts like he doesn't recognize her.

The woman who climbed the steps enters. She picks up the necklace and hugs him for the gift.

I don't know if the doctor is her husband.

The actress gets out of the chair and leaves unnoticed.

A critic wrote, "Did you ever hear of [an eye specialist], worth his salt, who would permit his wife to come into said office on a household errand while he was examining a patient? Can you imagine an eye specialist stopping his examination, while talking with his wife, leaving patient stranded in operating chair? Are patients usually admitted to the consulting and operating room by a maid, to await the doctor, and permitted to look over the tools of the trade while said doctor is being hunted up? And to complete their tale of sins, Vitagraph has a closing scene with a horrible lighting of midnight and spotlight, for which no one understands the reason and in which there is nothing told."[2]

NOTES
[1] Claudy, C.H. "The Unnatural Scene," *The Moving Picture World*, June 3, 1911, p. 1258.
[2] *Loc. cit.*

Treasure Trove, 1911

—With John Bunny and Helen Gardner

The pot-bellied actor's bulbous nose and I drive up in an open touring car. The backdrop is a painting of a Victorian cottage. I'm in a huge hat tied on with a scarf and a duster over a long dress over my hourglass figure. The nose knocks on the front door.

Two elderly sisters sob in the middle of the living room. They say they have to sell their antiques. A Revolutionary ancestor hid the family silver from British soldiers and they are broke.

I'm mad I was given such a small part so I'm going to steal the next scene.

I walk to the set's painted window, look at crystal vases and china bowls on the desk. I pretend to inspect a bowl with my opera glasses, pace back and forth to command the camera's eye. The nose lowballs the sisters' price.

Around the studio, he's arrogant. None of us like him, but he's popular with audiences who only see him on screen.

The following scenes don't include me. A ghost in a Revolutionary War uniform appears and the short sister follows him through a wall.

I love this new trick photography.

He points at the desk in the living room. The sisters dig through the papers. They find a letter and map. They dig up the treasure in the back yard and write a letter saying they aren't selling their antiques.

If I ever get such a small part, I'll be a bigger thief and I'm going to drive the car.

The Death of King Edward III, 1911

Directed by J. Stuart Blackton

—With Charles Kent and Helen Gardner

The grey-haired British king lies in a chair in his private apartment. The set is painted to look like interior castle walls covered with tapestries. Gold and silver goblets, plates and candlesticks inlaid with fake rubies and emeralds sit on heavy furniture. The embroidered band around my skull feels tight. I kneel at the king's side. My hands on his arm signal my love and faithfulness. I pour a "soothing" potion, the doctor couldn't convince him to drink, past his lips. His head drops, mouth falls open, body slumps. I lean over his soft wrinkled face. The body's eyes are shut. I pull his signet ring off his finger, slip it onto mine and break the third wall with a leer.

This is my first time playing the villain and I love it.

I wanted to steal from my miserable womanizing husband, but he spent all his money before I could get to it. I'm still married to the cad.

The king's hands are nude. The pockets of my embroidered gown are heavy with his other rings. The king groans. I leave him to die alone. The nobles and servants rush in and sack the chamber. The king wakes up and sees the emptiness. He shakes his fists in the air, tries to cross the room, but falls face-up on the floor. A young priest enters with a cross.

My husband is godless.

The king stretches out his pale hand and takes the cross, falls dead with it on his chest.

I want to play villain again.

Regeneration, 1911

Directed by Charles Kent

—With Helen Gardner, Miss Lewis, Alfred Hollingsworth, Helen Costello

"Words cannot express what this Vitagraph Life Portrayal will show at [Insert name of your local nickelodeon] under the direction of the capable management, which has won the patronage and approval of the best people of this city."[1] "A new player, Miss Gardner, takes the woman's part and gives bright promise of fine work."[2]

This is the first time my name is given in a movie review. Producers don't reveal the names of their actors, afraid we'll demand more money. The audiences want to know our names and of course actors want more money.

THE HULSEY THEATRES—
HIGH CLASS MOTION PICTURES[3]
HOME OFFICE OKLAHOMA CITY, OK

October 31, 1911

Miss Gardner:

I want to complement you on your acting in "Regeneration" as it is truly the swellest piece of acting all through I have ever seen in any picture, and I have seen a few. Been in this business and the theatrical business for ten years.

It is truly superb, and I want you to know that my audiences are pleased beyond any doubt. Believe me.

I am truly yours,
Mgr. Orpheum. St. H. Tuggle

INCIDENTAL MUSIC: As the mother and child are deserted by the father, the pianist should play "In the City Where Nobody Cares" (Chas. K. Harris).[4]

Vitagraph just started suggesting piano pieces for musical accompaniment to their films, but they expect the theatre to go out and buy the sheet music.

Living room scene. A man stomps out the door. The woman and child cry, reach out their arms to him.

Street scene. The woman dressed in rags sells pencils to passers-by. The thin child stands next to her, finger in her mouth. The woman slumps. She writes a note and pins it to the child's ragged dress. Intertitle: I AM THE WIFE OF HUNTER ROSS AND THIS IS OUR CHILD.

In a bar, Hunter Ross laughs and takes one drink after another. A woman with thick make-up dressed in tight lace and satin and swathed in necklaces drinks and laughs with him. He puts his arm around her. He rears back and strikes her. She rushes out.

I've never allowed a man to hit me and I never will. They cheat on me and lie, but I do it back to them. I don't like playing an abused woman on screen. It's ironic that the first time my name appears in a review I'm being hit, but I hope watching my character change her lifestyle will give abused women courage.

INCIDENTAL MUSIC: As the man strikes the woman, play "The Melody in F" (Rubenstein).

By a river, the mistress staggers to the edge. The wife of Hunter Ross lies lifeless on the bank, their child kneels beside her. Pencils are strewn on the grass.

INCIDENTAL MUSIC: As the mistress discovers the girl with hands reaching for her waist, play "Let Me Be Your Little Girl" (Harry Ennis).

Living room with satin curtains, velvet couches, lace doilies on tables. The mistress enters with the child and reads the note. Jaw set, she stands up straight and pounds her chest. She throws her cigarettes and whiskey into a wastebasket. Hunter Ross enters, takes his child from his mistress and leaves.

Dress shop. The mistress, dressed in a long black skirt and suit jacket, waits on customers. Ross enters, looks at her, smiles. They hug.

INCIDENTAL MUSIC: As the regeneration in the mistress' and Ross' characters is shown, play "And a Little Child Shall Lead Them" (Chas. K. Harris).

The sticky-sweet moral of the story is that redemption is possible when an innocent child leads. My daughter is innocent but she doesn't try to redeem me. I live in Brooklyn and keep her with my mother in Bridgeport. I wonder if she knows some of my biggest fans are children.

Albany N.Y.[5]

Nov. 11, 1911

Miss Helen Gardner
Vitagraph Moving Picture Co., New York City

My Dear Miss Gardner,

I hope I will not be asking two much if I ask you for your photo. I have seen you in many pictures, and I am always in hope of seeing you when I go to the moving pictures. I see you in "The Regeneration" the other day and I have simply gone crazy about you. I cannot tell you how much I love you, and I know I would love you much more if I knew you personally. You may know how much I love you if you have ever loved an actress when you were a girl of sixteen, but perhaps you were an actress yourself when you were that old. I wanted to write to you long ago, but I did not know your name until about a month ago, I was to New York and I see your picture outside of a Moving Picture Theatre with your name under it. I wanted to write a much nicer letter than this, but it seems as soon as I set down to write, I cannot write what I wanted too. I hope you will not think me silly for writing to you because I could not keep back any longer. I would be very, very thankful for your photo, if it was just a small one and I could say that, I got it from Miss Helen Gardner. Hoping to recieve one, I will remain one of your Albany friends

Sincerely
Isabel H. Andres
247 Elk St.

My eight-year-old writes me with spelling mistakes like Isabel's. Sometimes I send her a postcard back, but I need my independence. I tried to miscarry, get an abortion, but Hèléne's a sweet thing and I know she misses me, but this is my career in film.

NOTES

[1] "Regeneration," Vitagraph Press Announcements. Cut these out and send them to your Local Papers." *Vitagraph Life Portrayals*, October 17-November 1, 1911, v 1, #8, p 31.

[2] "Regeneration," *Moving Picture World, November 11, 1911, v. 10, #6, p. 469.*

[3] Huggle, S.T., "Miss Gardner," October 31, 1911, *Helen Gardner Vitagraph Scrapbook*, Dorin Schumacher personal collection.

[4] "Incidental Music Suggestions for Vitagraph Films, Regeneration." *Vitagraph Life Portrayals*, October 17-November 1, 1911, v 1, #8, p. 10.

[5] Andres, Isabel H. "My Dear Miss Gardner," November 19, 1911, *Helen Gardner Vitagraph Scrapbook*.

Dorin Schumacher's 2017 writing includes Brooklyn Rail, At Large, Fjords Review, Bridge Eight *and* Quiet Lunch. *Her writing on silent film star Helen Gardner appears in* Women Screenwriters *(Palgrave Macmillan, 2015), the* Encyclopedia of Early Cinema *(Routledge, 2010),* This Film is Dangerous *and many other anthologies and publications. Her personal writing appears in* The New York Times. *Her site is beacontowers.media*

Matt Hart

Philosophical Investigations

If a lion could speak, we couldn't understand him."
—Wittgenstein

A lion says a bunch of weird/perplexing things about the world
That he's a lion doesn't really matter, but he hopes some of you will know
his heart from what comes next   Furthermore,
that he's a king-of-the-jungle isn't necessary, which is different than saying
it doesn't matter   What's necessary is logically necessary,
or it's logically unnecessary, that is all   So he roars and roars

a bunch of enigmatic/technical things about the world,
and about its being a bunch of facts not things,
or about its being mostly of words
in some pianist's ivory throat   or not
The possibility of the negation of any fact is embedded
in the totality of facts as they present themselves, but

neither the totality, nor the possibility are part of what the lion says,
though what he says shows them in angelic frostbite
This he implies through singing a lot, the chaos of the soul
His singing is anomalous and sounds like polished oyster shells, feverish
and reticent, as if the totality of history has already been written
(potentially anyway), even before it attaches itself

to the mothership-garden of earthly delights   It wants to declare
and conclude itself—goodness and beauty, mercy and grace,
Paradise found and unmoored from itself   But history cannot
say such things, the lion knows—logically or sensibly with feeling, nor
accurately/scientifically with verve, minus loss   One can't say
feeling; one can only express it—rarely, "my dear," or falsely, "my love"

A moth settles onto my window ledge lost, light spilling in
on the book the lion wrote   Nothing is certain, but it seems
someone has leaned a ladder up against the house we don't share
together anymore, or much   Yes, I am here   I have always been
here   I am not very far   I climb into the canopy of trees,
and when I reach through their green, a hippopotamus

is in the room or a hippopotamus is not in the room   As always,
this is true   And all the light that ever warmed me is fading
rather mystically—fading into mountain sea—
with glitter-gloss and lion-ry—
and silence

Hit By a Deer

Too many skies
supermassive and defeated
                    The beer one
all up-in-arms, but rejected   The leaf one
almost empty, but for one falling robin
And someone in the wee hours,
who side-swiped my mirror,
scraped a red smear on the side of how I go
I forgive you, fair shadow
The car doesn't matter
I was parked on the street,
and the waves of rush hour will no doubt
still zoom up around me anyway,
whether I desire them to or not
        I don't
I am redolent with globular fruit
How to live and how not to in a clearing
                    of another sky,
                        the Blues one

Hello, dear saviors or devils,
I've arrived here for our meeting—
        with antlers
                bowls of custard
Can't keep flipping my wig like a judge
                    All the bright colors
                Cold limes and wreck reds
        All I have to say is love, I say
again and again
        but no fire begins, no spark

                              of an azalea
No pine tree face on the hill
                    sinks to ash
Instead, most of me floats
                    like something being nudged
from an ambiguous nest of clouds
Is this sky's blood worth spilling

                              myself

Is it ever vital moss
No, it's mess—

                    wonder and walrus
            plasma and plaster—
the cover that sustains me
when I wake up twenty times a night

                              mare

and yet still not awake   This new sky
I've started, I can't quite see it

                              through

Why finish anything ever if it's working
Why finish anything in love
until you have to

Poem in the Far Purple Reaches

Dear blear reactor
      dust
Waves of Lake Michigan
        Mountains of Vermont
           O charge and retreat
              of infinite repeat
Sweet peas and geraniums,
      your affectionate pink

                        armor
           I need it
Nowadays
bullets always cutting through the brown skins of butter
Eagles with their violence make carnitas on the lawn
And in this most horrible of dreamiest conditions,
      an old cigarette vending machine
         You know the sort
           if you're of a certain age
Drop in your change, then
      pull the plastic handle
         to make your kill/selection—
           black sheep black sheep
              a bolt goes through a heart
Now's the time
New works of love
The grace of God starts, as in startles, most of us
               Startles me most of all
The mercy of heaven
      may as yet extend through our lives, but only
         (right after this commercial)

                    like a YouTube channel
                        (please subscribe)
All Satanic beer bottle
The bird feeder raccoons
            I will scatter
                with Joe Strummer
Daddy was a bankrobber
Little gold fox blends its NOW against the sun
and Flakey Biscuit bellies-up to lay one on me
                                        good
I kiss a lot the air this year
            both red cheeks on a dime
                for a beer

Matt Hart is the author of seven books of poems, including Radiant Action *(H_NGM_N Books, 2016),* Radiant Companion *(Monster House Press, 2016), and* Blue Jay Slayer, *an art and poetry collaboration with artist Ken Henson (Aurore Press, 2015). Hart's poems, reviews, and essays have appeared or are forthcoming in numerous print and online journals, including* The Academy of American Poets online, *Big Bell, Coldfront, Columbia Poetry Review, H_NGM_N, Harvard Review, Jam Tarts Magazine, jubilat, Kenyon Review* online, *Lungfull!, and POETRY, among others. His awards include a Pushcart Prize, a 2013 individual artist grant from The Shifting Foundation, and fellowships from both the Bread Loaf Writers' Conference and the Warren Wilson College MFA Program for Writers. A co-founder and the editor-in-chief of* Forklift, Ohio: A Journal of Poetry, Cooking & Light Industrial Safety, *he lives in Cincinnati where he is Associate Professor in Creative Writing and the Chair of Liberal Arts at the Art Academy of Cincinnati. He plays guitar and shouts in the bands TRAVEL and THE LOUDEST SOUNDER.*

Vijay Seshadri

Immanence

In her memoir fragment *A Sketch of the Past*, Virginia Woolf says that until she wrote *To the Lighthouse* she was haunted by the memory of her mother, who had died when Woolf was thirteen. The writing of *To the Lighthouse*—Mrs. Ramsay, the main character, is based on Julia Stephen—was cathartic. It put the haunting to rest. Most writers understand the process. Memories, their mass bending and shaping inner space, exciting or oppressing the imagination, are suddenly given over through the act of writing to a mausoleum of words. They lose their force and their capacity to involve the psyche in themselves. Also, though, they lose their pungency and immediacy. Woolf implies that she felt relief and freedom when she put her memories to rest in her novel, but when I first experienced this catharsis I felt a sense of loss. The memory I purged by consigning it to the page was a painful one. Its stinging presence had been with me for so long, though, and revisiting it in my mind evoked the experience that it was a picture so precise, with such clarity and detail, that I was bereft when I realized that through its articulation its force had been drained.

I've written before about my first encounter with "O God Our Help in Ages Past," and about the imprint the hymn left on my mind. That writing, curiously, hasn't drained the memory of its force or erased the imprint. The imprint in fact seems clearer and more deeply etched every time I visit the chamber in my mind where it is located. It has also taken on new properties over time, uncanny properties. It seems to glow, and it illumines more brilliantly the fragmentary images and What I wrote about the hymn almost twenty years ago comes from one of my own memoir fragments. It is part of a story about immigration and dislocation and fraught assimilation into a new culture.

sense memories that surround it—and, amazingly, it illuminates fresh images, images that I don't remember remembering before, but that I now remember.

What I wrote about the hymn almost twenty years ago comes from one of my own memoir fragments. It is part of a story about immigration and dislocation and fraught assimilation into a new culture. At the very end of the 1950s, my mother and I were fetched from India by my father—he had been in America getting his Ph.D., in physical chemistry—and taken to Ottawa, where he assumed a postdoctoral fellowship with Canada's National Research Council. The memoir fragment's relevant passage, part of a description of the neighborhood we found ourselves in, is this one: "The people who lived around us were named Matherson, Campbell, Jones. Their religion was nonconformist and their game was ice hockey. I never took to the hockey, though I played a lot of it. I possessed a talent for the religion, though. My parents had the residual piety that characterizes even the most agnostic Indians of their generation, and a God-is-a-diamond-with-many-facets attitude toward doctrine. When the mother of a friend of mine asked if I could accompany him to Sunday school, they said yes, and I became a valued member of a Christian congregation. I might have been valued because I was seen as a heathen ripe for conversion, but I doubt it. Those people were generous and unintrusive and enlightened. They had a reticence and dignity appropriate to their climate and dispensation. I'm sure they liked me as much as they did because I was a loud and contented hymn-singer, and almost letter perfect in learning the Bible stories. My favorite story was the one about Joseph, who was depicted in our Bible reader wearing his coat of many colors while his jealous brothers circled around him, getting ready to throw him into the pit. My favorite hymn was 'O God Our Help in Ages Past,' whose first stanza,

O God our help in ages past,
Our hope for years to come,
Our shelter from the stormy blast,
And our eternal home.

still calls up for me an image of sticklike, barely discernible human figures toiling over an immense, featureless landscape."

This account, with its quick sketch of my parents, its understated ironies, and its details of social history, is not the account I would give now of this moment in my life. My father and my mother both passed away recently, and their deaths have not only left me alone with our once shared memories but altered the meaning of those memories. When I first told this story, I told it as if it were about our finding our way in a new world. If I told it today, I would dispense with society and with the social details. I would linger in the vision the hymn gave me, which in the aftermath of losing my parents seems to be suffused, mysteriously, with the love I have for them. I would paint a picture of that landscape, which is no longer featureless in my imagination. It seems, rather, like an immense flow of rust-brown igneous rock, scored and grooved and fissured with semicircles. And the sticklike figures, which I see far below me, are now in my imagination recognizably ourselves. My parents had made an immense leap of faith in coming to this continent when they did, when no one from their ancient South Indian world was ever disposed to leave it, especially to go so far, to a place so strange to their habits, understandings, their sense of social order. They had left one

> They had left one civilization for another and for long, suspenseful years were caught between two contrived human constructs, suspended over the abyss of reality.

civilization for another and for long, suspenseful years were caught between two contrived human constructs, suspended over the abyss of reality. When I hear "O God Our Help in Ages Past," when I spool it out in my mind, they seem somehow to live inside the hymn. The power of its petition seems to invest them with an absolute reality, and for my part I can almost feel myself in the middle of that leap of faith, in all its terror and exhilaration.

Vijay Seshadri is the author of three collections of poetry, including 3 Sections, *which was awarded the 2014 Pulitzer Prize for Poetry. The Pulitzer Prize committee praised* 3 Sections *as: "a compelling collection of poems that examine human consciousness, from birth to dementia, in a voice that is by turns witty and grave, compassionate and remorseless." His other collections include* The Long Meadow, *which won the James Laughlin Award, and* Wild Kingdom. *His poems, essays, and reviews have appeared in* AGNI, the American Scholar, Antaeus, Bomb, Boulevard, Lumina, the Nation, the New Yorker, the Paris Review, Shenandoah, Southwest Review, Threepenny Review, Verse, Western Humanities Review, Yale Review, the Times Book Review, the Philadelphia Enquirer, Bomb, San Diego Reader, *and* TriQuarterly, *and in many anthologies, including* Best American Poetry.

Christopher Collins

Lesson

Finishing the grass, I found
      your white silk splayed

along the groove of an aluminum
      water gutter,

and stopped my finger
      from touching your body—

glistered black, live,
      the red hourglass

on your belly, tattoo
      of power and poison.

I called my kids out
      from the house, their eyes

squinting with bent bodies
      as you posed before us,

your slightest advance
      pimpling our flesh.

To them I described
      your markings,

instructed them
      you are to be revered,

never touched
      with bare finger or foot,

to be killed, swiftly—the scraping
      of my sole separating

the beautiful black pieces
      of your body.

Passing the Neighbor's Lawn

"Dandelions
        are lawn-stains,"
our neighbor yells, but

for my daughter, her voice—
                    how she

squeals from my hand
        to blow
                a hundred wishes
                        into the sky—

makes each white seed head
spotting the neighbor's backyard lawn

        a nature's blemish
well worth having.

Sleeping with Animals

This evening, as a summer storm
rives the night sky, our bed

becomes the shelter-house
for our son and his pets—

two Labradors, their pup,
one, brown-spotted kitten.

Again he wakes from thunder,
or is it the blood

that seems to seep below
his bed's dust ruffle? I sense

his body postured
before my face—lip

tucked tensely below
front teeth, his inanimate

animals and blue blanket
being towed by shaking hands.

My wife quietly complains
of room as he burrows

between us—hair matted,
body pajama-damp—positioning

his animals head-to-foot
in a bulwark for protection.

And as the storm settles
so does he as we slept, our arms

interlaced below thick blankets,
his breath and mine cadenced

in drops of rainwater
fading with the distance.

Christopher Collins earned his M.F.A. in Creative Writing (Poetry) at Murray State University. He is a former Captain having served twelve years in the U.S. Army (Reserve). He completed three combat deployments in Afghanistan and Iraq as a platoon leader and as a commander. He has published one poetry chapbook entitled Gathering Leaves for War *(Finishing Line Press, 2013).* My American Night, *winner of the 2017 Georgia Poetry Prize from UGA Press is his first full-length poetry collection to be published.*

Ashley M. Jones

Hoghead Cheese Haiku

My dad would slice it
over crackers, each sliver
a gravelly gray—

hog's head boiled down, too
flat to recognize as hog
anymore—now, souse—

we ate it—joy spilled
like salt between our fingers,
like hog between them—

this meal, so special
because Dad made it for us,
a secret treasure—

we did not know these
meals: hoghead cheese, canned sausage,
rice and rice and rice,

told us we weren't rich—
we thought, delicacy, treat,
what steak could top this?

and what magic lies
within a pig's head, pig's foot,
this, unnatural

dairy, this gray cheese
made of snout, flesh, feet, and heart—
congealed, sour art.

My Grandfather Returns as Oil

—after Marci Calabretta Cancio-Bello

His face is thick, unseeable—
I only catch glimpses in my dreams,
in the shadows falling, thickly, on my father's face.
They say he was mean,
smothering like oil,
like its slick, tight grip on water,
like a hand pressed to a closing throat.
I only knew my grandfather
through stories, through the darkness
seeping out of my grandma's tender eyes—
        her smile, the old easy chair, the love wrapped between her swollen
fingers—
but her children knew him
as the throbbing print of his hand on her cheek,
on her nose, just soft enough to break,
through the snake of the extension cord, crashing,
thundering through their skin.
Grandfather, is that your blood creeping through my heart—
        rage, viscous and unyielding, crude and dangerous as oil—
or do you already sit on my skin, spreading, quickly,
silently covering me in your persistent, glossy shadow?

Racists in Space

"Nobody wants to go back to that crazy racist life."
"No, nobody wants to go back to riding a horse and buggy."
"No, we not going back to that. People trying to go to space."
———pulled from a conversation with my parents

Meet George Jetson—his Klan robe is made of supersonic polyester—Jane, his wife, bakes space cookies for Mr. Spacely, the Grand Space Dragon. They host dinner parties, and Rosie the Negrobot sings the old cotton songs.

A space joke: How many niggers does it take to make a Spacely's Sproket? None, cause ain't no niggers in space. We left them in steamy Alabama, in the hills and trees of Virginia back on Earth.

Here, we breathe in little clear bubbles fastened around our necks. Curious, we think, these tourniquets that save our space-aged lives. Curious, we think—we used to fasten a bubble of air, a rope around a black man's neck, called it a noose and waited till the air crackled out of his body. How much faster he'd implode in space, how quickly his body would turn inside out to greet the gaping black.

Ashley M. Jones received an MFA in poetry from Florida International University. She received a 2015 Rona Jaffe Foundation Writers Award, and her debut collection, Magic City Gospel, *was published by Hub City Press, and it won the silver medal in poetry in the 2017 Independent Publishers Book Awards. She teaches Creative Writing at the Alabama School of Fine Arts.*

Sofie Harsha

Mute Button

I.

Liam puts her shoes in the box. All the tennis shoes together smell of worn rubber and wet canvas. He knows she buys everything at thrift stores so there's that smell too—a collection of random years, places, people, all convened together in a pile of shoes. When he grabs an armful of her high heels to transfer into the box, their sharp edges dig into his arms as if trying to make him remember them later.

Pedra watches TV facing away from him as he packs her things, the top of her head peeking up over the frame of his couch. Her head is so dark and small, like a soft burrowing animal. Pedra is so goddamn small. If he didn't know exactly who was sitting on the couch facing away from him, he'd think it was a child.

Unfortunately the heels' points and wedges keep Liam from shutting the box completely. They protrude from the box as if trying to escape. *The amount of space I perceive high heels to take up is misleading,* he thinks to himself, and almost vocalizes this thought to Pedra. She might find it funny, the phrasing. He'd like to hear her laugh. He hasn't heard her laugh for over a week, when she laughed so loudly at one of her shows the sound had traveled upstairs to his room.

He thinks of moving the high heels to a second box so they'll fit, but it doesn't really matter. A generous amount of tape has always worked for him when boxes won't shut.

Pedra watches TV facing away from him as he packs her things, the top of her head peeking up over the frame of his couch. Her head is so dark and small, like a soft burrowing animal. Pedra is so goddamn small.

As he goes to grab another box from the garage, this one for her books, he reminds himself again that Pedra needs to go. As a roommate she is no longer viable. She hyperventilates in her sleep every night and in the morning retells the nightmares as if they've really happened. As if she's really attacked every night by the same man. And she screams at him in Spanish when they drink together. Things he can't understand.

Te amo tu puto! Idiota! Tu niño estupido. Por que? Porque. Por que? Porque. Porque.

> She hyperventilates in her sleep every night and in the morning retells the night-mares as if they've really happened. As if she's really attacked every night by the same man. And she screams at him in Spanish when they drink together. Things he can't understand.

There was also that time she looked across the table at him two months ago, right in the eye, and whispered, I wanna give you a blow job. When he hadn't answered her, she kept speaking, so soft and lilting. I want to fall asleep on your chest playing with your pelotas. I want you to come on my face. On my stomach. In my ass. Quieres?

It all makes him very uncomfortable.

Pedra doesn't talk to him anymore, even when he walks up behind her constant spot on the couch and stops a while, arms crossed. A friendly pause in his day to watch TV with her. He usually says something like *What is this show? It's ridiculous.* In the past she's either laughed or given him a witty reply, but for a month she's chosen to ignore him or nod in agreement. Or disagreement.

She hasn't looked in his direction all morning, though the house is now nearly empty of all her things. He's been packing her stuff throughout the night and into the cold early morning dawn. The morning sky was almost lavender, almost sickeningly so, when he'd finally taken a break to make himself breakfast and noticed that Pedra had fallen asleep on the couch drunk again. When he heard her murmur softly awake, he thought she would come talk to him. He thought for sure she would. Especially when he started singing to her pet rabbit, Lolita. He'd chosen one of his childhood songs, "Sandy Man Sammy." Lolita had seemed to enjoy it, but Pedra hadn't said anything, hadn't even laughed. She'd just clicked the TV on and commenced staring, wide-eyed like a slowly dying deer.

Liam chalks it up to the TV. She seems to be really enjoying her stand up specials and crime shows lately. Very immersed.

The top of Pedra's head, buoyed over the couch, hasn't moved in an hour or so and he wants to walk around the couch to make sure she's okay or to see her face. Every time he looks at Pedra's face he's reminded of the very important fact that he needs her to move out. The lips especially. Full and small at the same time. Her face is terrible and she is always yelling or crying at him with it. Or screaming silently while she sleeps. Actually he doesn't know for certain that she screams silently while asleep, but it's what he always imagines when she wakes him up with her hyperventilating from the room directly below his. In his mind, her whole face a boundless scream.

He'll have to pack up her TV soon. Liam is trying to be respectful of her TV time, but he also doesn't want to accidentally keep the thing when he moves her out of their house. He isn't a thief. He's taken her mosaic coffee table to his truck already, pulling it directly out from under her resting feet. When he took the table, Pedra had just continued watching her show, keeping her glass of water at her side, stretching her legs out in front of her on the floor as if nothing had changed. Liam wouldn't have been surprised if she'd kept her legs suspended in midair, resting them on an invisible table.

The house is so damn empty, the blue carpet a large ocean of stains. He'd never noticed the stains before, but now that the house is empty they're all over the place.

Pedra also hadn't paid attention when he took all her art off the wall and wrapped the frames in her sheets. She didn't say anything when he took her still-dirty cereal bowl out of her soft, limp hands and put it in a box with the rest of her kitchen supplies.

Things to pack are running out, boxes stacked high against the entryway wall, some already in his truck. Liam will definitely have to make a move for the TV soon.

The house is so damn empty, the blue carpet a large ocean of stains. He'd never noticed the stains before, but now that the house is empty they're all over the place. Liam has never seen a still-occupied house so empty and so full of stains. Come to think of it, everything, stained and unstained, belongs to Pedra, except the couch she's sitting on. He'll have to get new furniture.

She will forgive him. And in her new apartment, wherever that is, she can watch TV all the time. Any time of day. He'll remind her of that when he drops her off at her brother's.

Liam has already called her brother, Patricio, to tell him the plan. Patricio had sounded confused. Groggy. It had taken him a bit to switch from Spanish to English. But at least Patricio is aware now that his sister is moving into his apartment for a little while. Just until she finds another place. Today is the day.

Liam is almost out of boxes.

II.

Watching *Forensic Files* calms Pedra. It affirms her hypervigilance and makes her recurring nightmares seem wholesome by contrast. In every episode everything gets wrapped up. Solved. Through science. It's comforting. In fact, science is always comforting, especially when you're trying to sleep your days away. When things make sense it's easier for Pedra to sleep.

All the murder cases on *Forensic Files* are years and years old, almost as if nothing bad ever happens anymore. Liam says that according to *Forensic Files*, everyone who solves crimes has a mustache.

This morning's episodes of *Forensic Files* are entirely mustacheless.

Pedra loves it when Liam is wrong.

Pedra loves it when Liam is right.

Pedra loves hearing Liam shuffle around the house in his slippers. She loves his face in the morning. She hates his face at night.

Pedra feels like a ghost, but heavier. A ghost with only skin and a heart.

Pedra loves Liam.

Liam does not return her feelings.

Ever since he told her so a week ago, the house has felt emptier, now just a hollow space she inhabits because she has to. Because she is there and the house is there, walled all around her.

Pedra feels like a ghost, but heavier. A ghost with only skin and a heart.

Every time Liam asks her for a ride somewhere or to go out laughing on the town, she wishes she could send another version of herself in her place. One without a heart. One without ache. One without guts. One as hollow as their house now that he's told her she means very little to him, maybe as much as a piece of furniture. A couch. A table. Something used and replaceable.

The house seems emptier than ever.

If she could cry while awake anymore Pedra's certain she would be crying now, watching the girl on the screen talk about how her sister would never hurt a fly. How the pain never goes away. Watching the girl as she says how terrible it is. How terrible it is that her sister had to die that way.

III.

Respectfully, Liam waits for the commercials to switch off the TV. He shimmies it from its mount, and stands for a moment in front of Pedra with it hulking in his arms. She continues looking past him at the bare mount as if the TV is still on, her eyes blank and empty.

Pedra?

She doesn't answer him.

Pedra? I called your brother and he said he's leaving his door and the door to his storage unit open for you. You're moving out today. I've got all your things packed. Triz knows you're coming.

Pedra's delicate face is completely deserted and suddenly Liam wants to kiss her on her forehead, just to put something there. But the TV is getting heavy and he knows exactly where to wedge it in his overflowing truck. Except for the remote still in her hand, the TV is the last item.

It's time.

She can carry Lolita in her lap in the truck. It'll make her smile. She will forgive him.

Pedra, come on, talk to me, he says as he moves toward the door with her TV.

Pedra doesn't answer him.

Out in the truck, the TV doesn't fit where Liam had planned. He sets it on the cold grass of late winter. He'll have to move some things around. Maybe the wedging was a bad idea in the first place. The TV will be safer in a box. He could even find some bubble wrap.

When Liam enters the garage, he notices a box he missed before, leaning next to the push lawn mower. Its largeness startles him. The box is taller than he is, and wider, almost as if sometime over the course of the day the lawn mower had created a box big enough to contain itself.

Perfecto! Liam imagined the lawn mower saying when it had finished. Perfecto.

Liam is ecstatic. An energy he doesn't usually have this time of winter shoots through him and he almost claps in an audience-like pre-encore ecstasy.

The box is everything Liam didn't know he needed.

He goes back to his truck and contemplates the four boxes of Pedra's books he's stacked in the middle seat. He's sweating in the mid-afternoon chill when the last of the four boxes is out on the lawn, next to the TV. He's sweating when he reclines the two front seats back as far as they'll go.

Pedra is still clutching the remote and staring at the spot where the TV had been when Liam comes back inside.

In the kitchen Lolita gives his arm a little sniff when he picks her up. Lolita has the funniest rabbit nose, pink with spots of brown. He likes it when she sniffs him.

The rabbit settles into Pedra's lap nicely and doesn't make a move to run away.

For what seems like the first time today, Pedra moves. She lifts the hand that isn't busy white-knuckling the remote and places it on Lolita's back. She pets her three times and then stops.

For Liam, it is enough.

Okay, hold her tight, Liam says, and bends to pick Pedra and the animal up in his arms.

Pedra does as he says.

As Liam carries Pedra out to the truck, Lolita in tow, he notices Pedra is only slightly heavier than her TV. So goddamn small. She stays quiet and leans her head against his shoulder, almost like a sleeping child about to be put to bed.

Out in the yard, it's gotten colder, even though the sun is at its peak. After the earlier lavender of the morning sky, Liam had forgotten to keep looking up at it. He didn't really think it could get better than the lavender. With Pedra and Lolita in his arms, he looks up now. The sky is so orange, and quickly fading into pink. He makes

As Liam carries Pedra out to the truck, Lolita in tow, he notices Pedra is only slightly heavier than her TV. So goddamn small.

a plan to sit outside and watch the sky change when he gets back.

Pedra and Lolita fit perfectly inside the box. And the box fits perfectly inside the front seat of his truck. Everything is working out. When Liam finally adds her TV to the box, he's careful not to hurt Pedra or Lolita with any of its sharp edges, and after he closes the large box, only a tiny part of the TV's base protrudes. Nothing tape can't fix.

The pink sky opens up to Liam on the highway toward Patricio's house, and he smiles quietly to himself the entire drive.

From inside the box, Liam hears Lolita scraping at the cardboard corners. He listens for Pedra, imagining her face in mid-scream, or mid-cry. But Liam can't hear Pedra at all.

Sofie Harsha is an amateur writer, musician, artist, comedienne, and screenwriter but says all the words after amateur as mostly jokes. Though originally from Minnesota, she recently became an official resident of North Carolina and has the paperwork to prove it. For work, she teaches fiction and poetry to 6th graders, provides tech support for faculty, and sometimes designs T-shirts for friends and family, pro bono. Find her at sofiewrites.com.

Wendy Oleson

Love Poem

Buckle up for another story about forbidden gin
with a quick mention of the cleavage-ogling dogs
in the parking lot of the Walgreens where I bought red
lipstick in order to look like you, Courtney Love.
I had the platinum wig, smeared liner, ripped fishnets—signs
of your general badass, crazy, cork-screwing-

self coursing through me en route to Marianne's party. Screw
everybody, I'm thinking, who won't bathe me in gin—
especially the girl who flashes a stoplight peace sign
because I'm so cool. Sigh. At Marianne's even the dog
ignores my entrance, despite my bag of booze, an IPA loved
by the host's husband. Yeah, I only brought beer, but I'm ready

for something harder (gin) and Marianne can read
it on my scowl. I sip her *smells-like-martini-spirit*, say, *Screw
with Kurt's memory at your peril, bitch*, but we laugh, and I love
her because she winces when I say *bitch*. So I say it again,
deeper, scratchier, more pavement-licking-like. The dog
(an honest-to-god bitch) sniffs my plastic pumps, a sign

she hasn't (has?) had that lobotomy, a sign
my feet stink. I work on my sweet 'tini drink, a RedVine
swizzle stick haunting the murky gray-green—a sign
Bitch went all out. But nobody's even a little screwed
or screwing, and this martini has no goddamn gin
(just Russian shit and Mountain Dew). Like a good dog

I lap it up, and even though she's never had another one,
after two more 'tinis I say *Where's the other dog? Dog is love,*
dammit. Somehow Dee walks in, Tanqueray in hand, and screws
one on for me: she pours and pours and I wanna scream
and drink until I'm on the floor, but before I can rage in red
lipstick scrawl on M's bathroom mirror: *bitch, I love you/gin,*

I'm on the floor again. The dog won't come, a bad sign,
I guess. Do I love or hate us, Rose White, Rose Red?
Whichever, it's just me screwed again, swimming in gin.

Drunk Watching *Celebrity Haunting*

Spirits will resort
to drastic measures.

They seek
resolution,
redemption,
Just like us,
the psychic lady says.

In the attic
bedroom
of a haunted
recording studio, Carnie Wilson's
grandpa
touched her
from the other side, yanked
the bedsheets
from her legs, sent
electric
currents
like a thousand needles
through her skin.

Why?

Carnie wants
to put the pieces together
because her life
no longer
fits.

Was Grandpa a bad man? A pervert?
the psychic has to ask.

No.

Then maybe
he wanted
to help.

There's nodding, tears.

He was saving you—

—From myself, and Carnie knows
to cool it with the booze.
She's gotta
be there
for her baby.

In the blue
light of Grandpa's
ghost, I finish
the bottle.

A good
reenactment, I believe,
my grandpa
also
liked gin.

Bob

Bob lives by the laws of Lacan, already seeing death in the seeds of his pleasure, the end beginning anything wonderful. Bob's like the folk singers of my youth, lesbians who trotted out lines from Shakespearean sonnets, who moaned about dying love or love unblooming. What isn't *consumed by that which it was nourished by?* The sun? The stars? Sigh. Those ladies weren't wrong to sing love's swan song, but it can be a little much—like it's becoming for you, Bob. Or me, because I don't want to see you unhappy, and I don't know if that guy, redolent forest of your pine, will ever let you *take him in hand.* You're glad to imagine it. Before sleep. Upon waking. Which might be enough. Still, I want things to work out—even if you don't need them to, Bob.

Wendy Oleson is author of Our Daughter and Other Stories, *winner of the 2016 Rachel Wetzsteon Chapbook Award (Map Literary). Her stories, poems, and hybrid texts appear or are forthcoming in* Crab Orchard Review, Passages North, Calyx, Copper Nickel, *and elsewhere. She teaches for the UCLA Extension Writers' Program and Washington State University. Wendy lives in Walla Walla, WA with her wife and their irrepressible dog, Winston.*

Anis Mojgani

Outside the quarry

I do not know that I can go into myself today
it feels of a child strung
between the wonder of a small frog—
soft & wet in the hand—& the want
of the fingers closing around
its tiny & beating heart
tightening in
until bursting
please do not push me
into one direction or another
I want to watch the clouds move
on the other side of the Asheville trees
a song without notes
the world around me
keeps my body singing
the outside of itself to the inside of itself
I want to stay on the porch of my heart
to not go into its shifting light—to hold the rocks
in my hand—to not have to crack them open
using the skulls in the cabinets
to not find out which of the two
is made of a harder thing
so speckle me wind
dress me in your warmth
touch my arms the hair of my youth
were that I was inside
in a room with windows
were that I was kissing or being kissed
by a something

closed & glowing with the day
limbs of honeysuckle
in the sun of the staircase
this quiet mouth sipping
upon a jug of yellow blossoms

On the bayou

the gentleman of lost marbles keeps showing up
asking me if I have seen anything resembling his voice

he gestures to the crates behind him and also asks
if any of what he has looks familiar

I tell him *I do not know*
I have lost a lot of things

the bayou always returns to me
even with never being steeped in it

too far up or down on the body of the river
to speak the cyprus tongue

I have little use for my swords
I only wish soft tigers who speak to other tigers

in the language of tigers
our hearts found one another

under the branches of a large and glowing tree
you walked me into the sunlight

decided then that this light was too warm on your skin
went inside thought me wanting to share space with you

was me giving myself up
I keep trying to crack the code

decipher our love
in hopes that it might reveal the textures that remained—

you had a book of birds from around the world
you held the book in your lap I sat next to you

the rain outside kept the world at bay
I touched the feather of an American goldfinch and you

felt a shiver under your kneecap
you dogeared the page of a Chilean flamingo

and the blood in me rushed south
I wanted to—
but—

the plates were old but such colors—
even with never having been—

the red tip of South America was—
was the same as the tip of your red tongue

Monsters of Roses

Cover me in open roses
in monsters of roses

Dawn falls like a spoon out of my hands
into a pan of water
between laughter
and the world is a wall
that the golden arms of laughing
punch through

If you find me on the roof of a house
with my shirt off
screaming into the enlarging day
I am only making visible my many invisible hearts

Anis Mojgani is the author of four poetry collections, all published by Write Bloody Publishing: The Pocketknife Bible *(2015),* Songs From Under The River *(2013),* The Feather Room *(2011), and* Over the Anvil We Stretch *(2008). He is a two-time National Poetry Slam Champion and winner of the International World Cup Poetry Slam. A TEDx Speaker and former resident of the Oregon Literary Arts Writers-in-the-Schools program, Mojgani has performed for audiences as varied as the House of Blues and the United Nations. His work has appeared on HBO, NPR, and in such journals as* Rattle, Paper Darts, Forklift, Ohio, *and* Used Furniture Review.

Elena Karina Byrne

The Future is a Beast Prelude

> *Rhythm is naturally less reliable on the side of the future. Between yesterday's nothingness and tomorrow's nothingness there is no symmetry. The future is but a prelude…*
> —*Gaston Bachelard*

Violence is commissioned in the instant the drinking game
hasn't yet happened. Life after death comes
before wedding rice is thrown over the shoulder
instead of salt. I want to free myself, but can't. There's an episode
called duration and it is embroidered under the bed
that belongs to daylight.
So, let us begin by saying there is a fact-accident, a continual
horizon lifted on the androgynous voice
     of the seagull suffering for food. The hull

of waves rises and falls whether it is day or
night, yesterday or today, without
permission. But the aim
is nothingness, the motionless hour nothing
is taken from us, meaning future.
"Within the *smiling regret*" of the past
is Baudelaire's cat's eye, yellow-lit
from within. All we have
to do is wait. Metronomic on the lake, I know
a duck hunter's decoy won't sink in the rain. Dead, Father still
    opens the door for Mother in the dream,
    half singing.

Self Portrait as Counterpart Always, Wait

                    and see. Wait and see.
Mother said only once and it was
easy to be poet, tongue

          field, before I was, the sex matchhead
          me, elevator matter of, greenery left
          out on cutting
          board after-smell, and I know I know lifted
limbs water-called up
before their name, pulse, lamppost and the all animal
kingdom come to me.
Skyfall.
Ozone's iris
          in the keyhole.

          Color stone star came to me
from the beaches, all those beaches, Mother
and crab shell inside-white
dull constellation, but I played
nothing to the story's departure from home, honing in on
you,
the obstacle we call beauty,
stumbled over
every time footing in the beast wake place
is always partly true.

          Flower thing.
I learned.

Run. Run there. You
estranged-returned-everything her, you
changed for yearn
            in the crave trade.
But, wait, face paint roll. And see.
The closest thing to
falling: Body
with twin fire escapes, hotel music
under the sea-flooded stairs of the last house.
                Hear it?
                Time turns it back over
to you.
The only mathematician's scissors
and surrealist's origami paper,
one child's hand coffin
            full of fresh crayons,
melting, forensic scientist's clock-face
at once kept away from
all of them.

Bring with You St. Joesph's Aspirin

Sore mosquito throats, Tomboy fever, unknown cat allergy colds. I was a sickly child. You could say a child outgrows such things as fever, mounts a metal stool, believing it a horse in Arizona, her headdress, Indian. The family tree still bends center with every battlefield wind there. Jury and judge, you're going to die. Spider's pale body husk shell is crushed beneath the dining room rug,—the Pinto horse running, running for the hills and the moon's skull moves out like salt-dissolve onto winter's hard snow road alone, again.

Mother's favorite people were doctors. Her mother, a Christian Scientist, let God decide when the bone cancer broke her left arm, steadying herself the third to bottom step home. Who hatched this unexplainable thing we call health knew nothing of what comes next. There's an imagined shiny red purse that appears and disappears between both mother and daughter at different times during the dying. No one can explain why. The psychic field is not acknowledged here. The purse is shiny and red and the horse is running like a battlefield wind away. The American tragedy is still an unhappy ending that sounds like fun.

Elena Karina Byrne, author of Squander *(Omnidawn 2016),* MASQUE *(Tupelo Press, 2008), and* The Flammable Bird, *(Zoo Press 2002), former 12 year Regional Director of the Poetry Society of America is a multi-media artist, editor, Poetry Consultant/Moderator for* The Los Angeles Times Festival of Books, *Literary Programs Director for* The Ruskin Art Club, *and one of the final judges for the Kate/Kingsley Tufts Prizes in poetry.*

Her book reviews and poetry publications, among others, include the Pushcart Prize XXXIII, Best American Poetry, Poetry, The Paris Review, American Poetry Review, TriQuarterly, The Kenyon Review, Denver Quarterly, Colorado Review, Slate, Poetry International, Ploughshares, OmniVerse, Verse, Academy of American Poets Poem-A-Day, Black Renaissance Noire, *and* BOMB. *Elena just completed a collection of essays entitled,* Voyeur Hour: Meditations on Poetry, Art & Desire.

Erik Anderson

What I Owe

On Friday, August 10, 1979, a man named Scott Crain entered the Sun First National Bank in Dunedin, Florida, and for $37.50 bought a Series E Treasury Bond with a $50 face value, asking the teller to make it out to Eric Scott Anderson of 36 Silvermire Road, Brookville, Colorado, 06825. Six days earlier, a Saturday, I had been born in Danbury, Connecticut. My parents lived with my then two-year-old brother in a townhome in nearby Brookfield, where there is a Silver*mine* Road, although there do not appear to be townhomes at number 36. There is, moreover, no town called Brookville, Colorado, and the zip code listed designates a stretch of Connecticut between Bridgeport and Fairfield.

I don't have many memories of my great-grandfather, but the ones I do are vivid. I remember, for instance, a summer day in the mid 1980s—I can't precisely name the year—when we watched a baseball game together, probably the Cubs or White Sox, at my grandmother's cottage on Lake Michigan. I remember Grandpa Crain kept calling certain players a word I'd never heard before and which I learned, not long after, was an infamous slur. The moment came to mind again when, thirty-seven years after it was issued, I cashed in the bond for $219.18, a return on investment of $181.68. My mother had discovered it while sorting through her safe deposit box and, assuming it had been a birthday present gone astray, had mailed it to me. How would I spend it, she wondered. What would I buy? Driving home from the bank, that memory fresh in my mind, the money felt like something to abjure.

Most white people, writes Robin DiAngelo, author of *What Does it Mean to be White?*, first register race no later than five, and for my part I remember once asking my parents, as we moved through a vestibule in one of the Chicago museums, about a guard's skin, much as I asked them a few years later, on the day of that baseball game, about the word my great-grandfather had used. I recall, in the first instance, being told that the man in the uniform was no different than me. I recall, in my grandmother's cottage, being told never to repeat the word I had heard. These weren't the worst answers, but insomuch as they encouraged me not to acknowledge race, they were also woefully incomplete, and the willful blindness they encouraged lasted well into adulthood.

Then again, such blindness was emblematic of my upbringing. Throughout my childhood, we lived in exceedingly white towns, first in Connecticut, then in Michigan. Walter Payton and Mike Singletary, standouts from the '85 Chicago Bears, were household names, but there were otherwise no people of color in our lives. Surrounded as I was by white people, living in segregation, I had no reason to think that the differences skin engendered were not only significant but also measurable—in terms of life expectancy, relative wealth or poverty, rates of incarceration, access to education, and even in the cultural products we produce and consume.

Writing last year in *Salon*, for instance, I reported on the dearth of writers of color in my reading from the previous two years. In 2014, I read only nine books by writers who were not white; in 2015, I read thirteen. Given the number of books I read in those years (58 and 63, respectively), I was ashamed by the percentages. In the year to come—that is, 2016—I vowed, as I had the year before, to do better, not out of a bean-counting sensibility but to hold myself accountable for any implicit biases. Up until that point, it had been easy for me to ignore race (and gender and sexuality) in my intellectual life, to pretend that it didn't matter, at least not to me. The numbers told, or let me tell, another story—about self-reflection or its absence, about valuing or not valuing other voices, and about how inaction can be active, especially when it comes to race.

Because the process felt positive and empowering, the dismissive tone in the essay's comment stream surprised me. Why, some seemed to ask, should a writer's race matter? Isn't a good book just a good book? But a good book is not just a good book, of course, because what could a person possibly mean when she says a book is good? That it's entertaining?

That it doesn't require her to think? Or, on the contrary, that the book is entertaining *because* it requires her to think—to attend to the language, to the construction of the text, to the questions it raises? Without delving into the finer grain of what makes a book *good*—texturally, structurally, thematically—such evaluations are so nebulous as to be almost meaningless. Good writing is good writing for various specific reasons, some of which stem from the biases (aesthetic, intellectual, and otherwise) of the reader.

That a book might be *just* a book, moreover, isolated from the worldly phenomena that produced it, implies that the decisions one makes about (or in the creation of) books or music or movies don't really matter because it's not like they *represent something larger* about the world. On the contrary, that's exactly what they do. Each book is part and parcel of some portion of the world, and the world is not a white monolith, although if you aren't paying attention, if you're thoughtlessly consuming cultural products, it can certainly seem that way.

Race matters in reading, then, because race matters in the world. To borrow DiAngelo's key metaphor, race is the water we swim in, a defining construct and system that shapes our social relations. In this country at least, race can get you killed—by a cop, by a vigilante, in the crossfire, at the hands of avowed or subconscious white supremacists. No white person is innocent in the larger dynamic of subordination (i.e., racism) that sometimes leads to such violence, and even if I am not consciously exploiting that dynamic, there have undoubtedly been times when I've benefitted from

Race matters in reading, then, because race matters in the world. To borrow DiAngelo's key metaphor, race is the water we swim in, a defining construct and system that shapes our social relations. In this country at least, race can get you killed—by a cop, by a vigilante, in the crossfire, at the hands of avowed or subconscious white supremacists. No white person is innocent [...]

it, when my path through life was enabled by my whiteness. This is hard for many white people to admit, in part because it requires that we see ourselves as racialized bodies, as opposed to, you know, "normal" ones. It requires that we accept, or even just acknowledge, we are complicit in oppression we didn't create but which our lives perpetuate. Counting, for the record, has not resolved that complicity, nor can it, but it has helped to prevent it from flaring up. Counting reminds me that unhobbling oneself from the constraints of bias is grueling, perennial, necessary work.

In 2016 I read slightly fewer books than in 2014 or 2015, but the aggregate length of Elena Ferrante's Neapolitan novels may have something to do with that. Of the fifty-three books I read, twenty, or 38%, were by writers of color. Thirty-one, or 58%, were by women. I don't love the limited, binary way I'm reporting these numbers, as it elides many important distinctions, but I still derive some satisfaction from the upward curves that graphing these three years of reading would produce. I'm also vowing, again, to do better. And by *better*, I don't mean a year in which I read only books written by, say, Korean women writers. I mean broader. I want to think more deliberately about what kinds of inclusivity my reading represents—or doesn't. As I was compiling 2016's preliminary numbers, for example, I realized I had **As I was compiling 2016's preliminary numbers, for example, I realized I had not read a single book by an Arab writer in the previous year. Or the year before. Or the year before that.** not read a single book by an Arab writer in the previous year. Or the year before. Or the year before that. Both volumes of Riad Sattouf's delightful *The Arab of the Future* sat on my desk on New Year's Day.

I haven't instituted a blanket moratorium on reading white male writers, but I suspect I have a comparatively good handle on what it's like to be a white man, a straight, cisgender one at that. I know far less, by comparison, about what it's like to be an Iranian American woman, which is one reason why Solmaz Sharif's *Look* was the first book I read in 2017. The truth is that I am a little sick of white men, sick of catching myself acting like one.

When I hear that certain white men feel their voices aren't being heard, that the culture or the economy has left them behind, I think, ungenerously, *get over yourself.* The history of western civilization, and American history in particular, is largely the history of the triumph of white men. Even as individual fortunes vary, as a social group we continue to come out on top.

Which brings me to the real problem with Scott's money: I don't need it. I am in a position to be charitable while others need far more than my charity could provide. Equally iniquitous: my charity is voluntary. I am not obliged to care for or about anyone other than myself and those dearest to me, in part because I wasn't raised to value solidarity across class or race or gender lines—except, perhaps, when it came to my whiteness. Instead, I came to see myself primarily as an individual, someone who acts as opposed to someone who acts in unison, as part of a group, or is acted upon.

This may be why the more I thought about the $219.18 in my pocket, it occurred to me to donate the money, maybe to the NAACP. At the same time, I worried that any hypothetical donation might be a form of self-congratulation, that to symbolically reject the cash would be to insist on my blamelessness, as though I might exonerate and extract myself from my great-grandfather's faults. And I don't want to give Scott's money away, much less read more broadly, if the primary purpose or outcome is to reinforce a heroic feeling of superiority. There's no way to exempt oneself from history, but there has to be a way to slalom through it, to put one's life (as a writer, reader, and human being) to ethical use.

The truth is that my great-grandfather was a careless man. Careless enough to badly botch the details of his newborn grandson's address, careless enough to leave a loaded weapon lying around the house, [...]

Another vivid incident from my childhood may offer a glimpse of how one might do that, albeit in a roundabout way. When I was four or five, we visited Scott and his second wife, Verna, at their home in Florida. There was a pair of twin beds, I remember, maybe where my brother and I were meant to sleep, maybe where Scott and Verna slept.

The revolver was in the drawer of the nightstand between them. I must have thought it was a toy, which is certainly how I brandished it in the screened-in porch where the grown-ups were chatting. The way my parents tell it, a hush fell over the room when they saw the loaded weapon in my hands. My father walked over slowly and, in dulcet tones, disarmed me.

The truth is that my great-grandfather was a careless man. Careless enough to badly botch the details of his newborn grandson's address, careless enough to leave a loaded weapon lying around the house, and careless enough to call professional athletes *niggers* in front of a young child. He was as careless in his love for me as he was in his hatred for others, and more than anything else, this is the inheritance I want to reject in the windfall I've received. Which may also be why I've let the cash bulge in my wallet as long as I have: it's a small reminder, each time I slip it into my back pocket, that I need to move considerately through life—far more so, anyway, than white people have in the past. I don't want to be inattentive or reckless in the way I put this money back into the world, not because I want to exempt myself from blame but because it is the necessary tax on this particular inheritance. Thoughtfulness is what I owe.

The Mole

Near the top of my forehead, along the left side where I part my hair, I have a small mole a bit larger than a sesame seed. It isn't unsightly, and combed just so my hair usually covers it. I tend to see it only when, fresh from the shower, I'm putting in gel to make my hair look fuller than it is. I didn't always have to do this, didn't have to manipulate my hair's volume or the precise angles at which it fell. Up until very recently I didn't even know I had that mole. Now what it tells me, each time I see it, is that whatever desirability I possess is waning. I don't know whether I should be frightened about that, or sad, or relieved.

My wife is feeling this too, having turned forty this year. Probably she's feeling it more intensely than I am, given the pressures women face. She's vigilant about gray hairs and wrinkles, her weight, the fit of her clothes. I would spend nearly zero minutes of each day thinking about these things, except that my wife obsesses about all of them, so that even while I remain unconcerned about my own gray hairs and wrinkles she prods me on a daily basis to consider hers. We get older, I say at night when she's preening in the mirror. There's no use fighting it.

But then the next morning I get out of the shower and rediscover my mole. There's no chance my hairline is moving forward. No chance, either, that I'll find myself twenty-five again. My life is moving, as all lives do, towards death, and though with any luck I'm still a long way from that moment, signs of aging are beginning to show, however lightly, on my body.

I'm not bothered by the thought of my eventual expiration—not yet, anyway—but its increasing proximity also means the loss of youth, even if I've never really wanted to be young, especially when I was. I have an August birthday, and as a child I tended to be either the youngest in the class or near enough. I was so insecure about my age I used to lie about it. Until I was fourteen or so, many of my friends pretended to believe I was a year older than I was. Whatever age signified—maturity, wisdom, respect—I wanted it. Even when I no longer lied about my age, I was impatient to end my childhood, graduating from college, among other things, a semester early.

I suppose I felt, and feel, youth as an insult, even or especially when people have told me I look young, as happened the other day when I met a senior professor from another department and she said *you guys are getting younger and younger. No,* I wanted to respond, *older and older.* Instead I said, a little resentfully, that I'd been teaching at the college for five years.

Sometimes I see this resentment in my son too, as though to be young were humiliating. *You're not old enough,* we tell him when he asks to watch certain movies or to walk to school on his own. Because part of our job as parents, or so we've often believed, is to keep his ceiling of authority artificially low, I could see how, in a perceptive child like him, this could lead to feeling inferior, or else to raging against subordination. This, after all, was what irritated me in the senior professor's comment: under the guise of collegiality, she wanted to put me in my place. She seemed to be asking, in effect, *What the hell do you know?*

That I am no longer young, in spite of what older friends say, could be what troubles me about my mole, but it may also be that I've bought into the conflation of youth and beauty, and that the real lesson of my slowly receding hairline is that I find age, in keeping with my culture, to be ugly. There is some sense to this, even if it pains me to admit it. Forgetting for a moment that beauty is also socially constructed, that we are at all good-looking to begin with has to do with the propagation of the species. Attractiveness primarily means the ability to attract a mate. Its purposes are sexual in the strictest sense: they are about the selection and exchange of desirable traits. The flower fades because it has served its purpose in reproducing the plant.

In general, people are less attractive to me on the whole than they ever have been. Walking through a crowded civic space, Manhattan's High Line on a warm summer day, say, I see a lot of hairless apes.

My wife and I, too, have reproduced, and pollination is no longer the order of the day. A man may be biologically able to fertilize a woman's eggs throughout his life, but any man who wants to forestall that inevitable shifting of gears must be deluding himself into thinking he hasn't reached the middle age I'm now confronting. My mole means that the prime directive of my life, to the degree it ever was, is no longer procreative.

I feel that too in my physical responses to women. Whatever lust once raged through me—as it does in all, or most, of us—has modulated over time. That's as it should be—a promise on which every marriage is premised—but fidelity aside, the impulse has also deadened somewhat, not gone but muted. I'm more aware than ever of women as corporeal beings who, like me, shit and piss and bleed and die. In general, people are less attractive to me on the whole than they ever have been. Walking through a crowded civic space, Manhattan's High Line on a warm summer day, say, I see a lot of hairless apes.

At this point in our married lives, my wife and I are also having sex less often than we once did. This is something I hear repeated from many of our married friends, or rather that my wife hears from other wives. The husbands, for some reason, never talk about it, while the wives seem to want reassurance. How much is too much? How much is not enough? Then again, this is a busy time in our lives, raising our son and pursuing our careers. I'm not sure either of us really misses it, though my wife has more than once registered, pointing her finger only partially at me, missing the feeling of being desired. We're worn out at the end of the day, and we're not in the mood first thing in the morning. Maybe this will change as we continue to age. Maybe not.

The news from other parts of my body isn't exactly great either. Because I jog a few times a week and eat a vegan diet, I've been able to keep my burgeoning gut in check, but I find I'm also less able to drink, one of life's little pleasures, that my mind is foggier when I do and that it takes me longer to recover when I overindulge, the threshold for which is much lower. I have a couple of skin things that I should probably have checked out, one on my left foot and the other on my right shoulder, and because I never wore my retainers after undergoing orthodontia, I have a crooked bottom tooth that gives me trouble when the seasons change, and, what's worse, I haven't been the dentist in a decade. One of the consolations of my age is that I know myself well enough to know that I won't address any of these things until they truly become problems. This cuts both ways because by now I know better.

I am gentler and more accepting with those I love than I have been at any other time in my life, but I still often find it difficult to be kind and even harder to be patient.

I am gentler and more accepting with those I love than I have been at any other time in my life, but I still often find it difficult to be kind and even harder to be patient. These are skills I hope to live long enough to learn, and if I die at a youngish age one of my chief regrets may be failing to apply them fully. I'll have other regrets, like not having a second child, but I've also accepted that having regrets may be an inevitable outcome of a life. Living with regrets is another skill age is trying to teach me.

If I live twice as long as I already have, my hairline will probably be much farther back, unless it's nonexistent. If I'm moderately lucky, I'll still be in relatively good health and the planet's climate won't be totally unlivable. I can imagine, again with any luck, living another ten reasonably good years after that, but life after 85, if you're fortunate enough to live that long, rarely turns out that well. Beyond that lies my life as a corpse, and I'd prefer the worms to eat me.

On some unconscious level this is where my mole leads me each morning.

Other days, because I'm wired this way, when I'm combing the gel through my hair, I think of the other kind of mole, the burrowing one, and I wonder whether I've misread the message, wonder what kind of subterranean presence my mole is boring into me, or else what hidden passageways my receding hairline makes visible, is exposing even here. And sometimes I'm reminded of a summer day twenty years ago when my girlfriend and I tunneled into a shoulder-high bluff that had emerged on the beach that year, linking a thin strip of wet sand below to the softer sand above, where we laid our towels. Mary had made good progress on the horizontal stretch when she took over the vertical. I crawled into the space she had vacated and, almost immediately, several feet of sand collapsed on me.

> Youth, like beauty, can fool you into thinking you won't die. Because it's hard to imagine a good-looking corpse, or rather it hardly matters how one looks on the way to the undertaker's.

I remember hearing Mary's screams from under the sand, and I remember trying, and failing, as my mouth filled with dirt, to scream back. I felt tremendous pressure on all sides but also tremendous lightness as I began to lose consciousness. I remember, more vaguely, feeling the hands that grabbed onto the only exposed parts of my body, just below my calves. My mother says I was an easy baby, but this was a breach birth, delivered from my death by my frantic girlfriend and a man I had never seen before and would never see again. I thanked him, of course, but there really wasn't any way of saying what needed to be said, and when he walked away Mary and I sat quietly together on the beach, looking out at the waves, stunned by the power of the thing we didn't have words for.

Youth, like beauty, can fool you into thinking you won't die. Because it's hard to imagine a good-looking corpse, or rather it hardly matters how one looks on the way to the undertaker's. Having nearly been buried alive at seventeen, I should have been cured of this misapprehension, but life has its way of lulling you into complacency. Now my mole presents its daily reminder, and even if I'm not bothered by the message, that the messenger shows up every day adds insult to injury.

I'll admit that after having spent much of my life eager to grow older, I want time to slow down, to hold age in abeyance. My wife, sensing my disquiet, tells me she still finds me handsome, will always find me handsome. I suppose there's some comfort in the way she wraps her arms around me while she says this, the way I stop washing the dishes for a moment and, standing there at the sink, feel her breasts pressed up against my back. Eventually, though, she turns to clean the stovetop, and I'm alone with the remnants of her homemade ramen. I wonder, as I scrub a curry-stained pot, what will this life be like, now that the old one is over.

It's a vein I'm just starting to mine.

Erik Anderson is the author of three books of nonfiction: The Poetics of Trespass, Estranger, *and, most recently,* Flutter Point: Essays. *He teaches at Franklin & Marshall College, where he also directs the annual Emerging Writers Festival.*

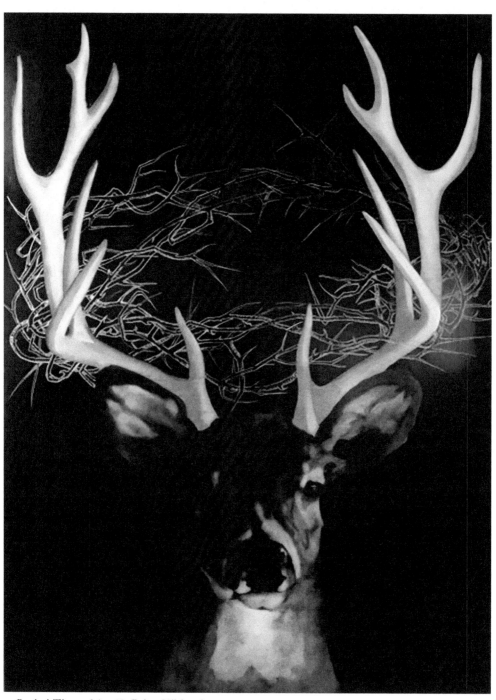

Buck &Thorns. 36 x 48. Brian Hibbard.

Buckhead 4. 48 × 48. Brian Hibbard.

Having a Ball 11. 48 x 48. Brian Hibbard.

Cow 4. 48 x 48. Brian Hibbard.

Counting Sheep 3. 36 x 48. Brian Hibbard.

h 280. 48 x 48. Brian Hibbard.

398. 36 x 48. Brian Hibbard.

Having a Ball 41. 40 x 40. Brian Hibbard.

Antler 4. 36 x 36. Brian Hibbard.

Aimee Nezhukumatathil

Love in the Time of Swine Flu

Because we think I might have it,
you take the couch. I can count on one hand
the times we have ever slept apart
under the same roof in our five years,

and those usually involved something
much worse than this sort of impenetrable
cough, the general misery involved
with dopey nausea, these vague chills.

But this time, we can't risk it—our small son
still breathes clear-light in the next room
and we can't afford to be *both* laid
up on our backs with a box of tissues

at our sides. Especially now that I carry
a small grapefruit, a second son, inside me.
In bed, I fever for your strong calves,
your nightsong breath on my neck

and—depending where we end up—wrist
or knee. I fever for the slip of straps down
my shoulder, I fever for the prickled pain
of lip-bite and bed burn. You get up and come

back to bed. We decide it is worth it. I wish
my name meant *wing*. The child still forming
inside me fevers for quiet, the silence of the after,
the silence of cell-bloom within our blood.

Travel Mommy Ghazal

Before I boarded the plane, my son sighs, *I wish I had another mommy*
with thirty-three teeth and she can be called: Travel Mommy.

We could sit by our fireplace and I can make hot cocoa
while the snow piles into pillows, but inside: *just Mom and me.*

That mother with a shiny extra tooth will sneak and fly and teach
poetry to big kids. Not my pretty, thirty-two toothed mommy.

But now I'm on the plane and searching the horizon for a prayer
to keep my family safe, something I learned from my own mom.

I find an answer in my coat pocket, a folded note my son sneaked
there while we waited at the ticket counter, addressed, To: Mommy.

Probably by the time you read this, Daddy is quiet and driving us home.
I aim my gaze to the almost-planets. *Isn't the sky colored like a parrot, Mom?*

Aimee Nezhukumatathil is the author of three books of poetry: Lucky Fish, *winner of the Hoffer*
Grand Prize for Prose and Independent Books; At the Drive-In Volcano; *and* Miracle Fruit. *With*
Ross Gay, she co-authored Lace & Pyrite, *a chapbook of nature poems (Organic Weapon Arts, 2014).*
She is the poetry editor of Orion Magazine *and her poems have appeared in the* Best American
Poetry *series,* American Poetry Review, New England Review, Poetry, Ploughshares, *and*
Tin House. *Awards for her writing include an NEA Fellowship in poetry and the Pushcart Prize. She*
teaches at The State University of New York at Fredonia, where she was awarded the Chancellor's Medal
of Excellence and named the campus-wide Hagan Young Scholar. In 2016-17, Nezhukumatathil will
be the Grisham Writer-in-Residence at the University of Mississippi's MFA program in creative writing.

Molly Ricks

The Last One Awake

I stayed up late, washed the dishes, bought time
until you came home.
I sleep better when you are home.

We lie in our beds, mine, a small fold out couch;
yours, as hard as floor, but you can sleep on anything.
I, cocooned by blankets and pillows;
you, covered by flannel and the quilt I made
when I was fourteen.
Though we yawned as we brushed our teeth
and went on about how sleepy we were,

our minds awaken once our eyes hit the ceiling
in the dark. We see our thoughts projected above us.
After some silence you ask *Are you awake?*
I answer *What's on your mind?* And you sigh

and tell me about dinner with Will and how he wants
to scare you away because he's so used to being alone
and you wonder what you should say to Whitney—who never
asks you how *you* are and I talk about how we can't

make others love us they have to choose
but we can tell them how they are making us feel
and leave it to them to connect the dots, make a change.
Aren't people so interesting, complex, different and the same
at the end of the day wanting to have meaning and be loved?

Do you think they lay awake at night talking like we do?

You've been thinking about the lines of a song—
something about life feeling like a dream—
because your life this year has felt like a dream and I say
life is but a dream. What is that from, life is but a dream?
I think it must be Shakespeare. It reminds you of a nursery rhyme.

In the quiet I realize we are both right.
Row row rowing gently down the dream within…

I am left, reading my thoughts on the ceiling,
cuddling into this familiar solitude.
The smallness of this talk has lulled you away from me.

Molly Ricks is the inaugural winner of the Thomas Lux Poetry Award from Georgia Tech. She graduated in 2017 from Georgia Tech with her degree in International Affairs and a certificate in Literature, Media and Communication. Along with writing and reading, Molly has a strong interest in Chinese culture and linguistics. She participated in an exchange to Renmin University in Beijing, where she studied Chinese Politics and Mandarin.

Stuart Dischell

Walking the Wall of Phillippe Auguste: Left Bank

Around the corner from my little studio, tucked inside the medieval city walls, I soon found Roger's bar, the Night Box, where I made friends among the staff and patrons who at times were one and the same people. A typical evening at the Night Box began as I passed on my way back from shopping, and Roger or Celina, the bartender, had propped open the door. If so, l stopped in for a *Pastis* or a beer. Evenings transformed quickly to late nights. An errant delivery boy, I wound up not bringing my groceries back to the studio. I put the food out on the bar, and we ate the cheese and bread and sliced meat and used the fruit to make drinks. Other times I went home by a different route, ate my supper, napped, and came back about eleven. The Night Box was supposed to close at two, but Roger would simply shut the door and we stayed as long as we pleased. Sometimes we went out in the neighborhood to after-hours bars and cellar clubs I could not always find again when by daylight I tried to reassure myself of where I had been.

Part British and French, Roger grew up mostly in Paris. Formerly a highly ranked tennis player, he retained the trademark youthful aggressiveness of a John McEnroe. His hair is a volatile red and his skin pale from staying up late in his bar and sleeping into the days. I heard one of his French friends call him in English, "The Rooster." "Roger the Rooster." He bought the bar from the former owner because it had been his hangout, and he was afraid it would close. Roger was still the best customer at the Night Box. He was his own guest and host.

Much banter was at hand. Hilduin, one of the regulars, known for his acerbic wit, told me one night, "We are being very boring. Let's talk to other people for awhile then meet again in forty minutes and tell each other what we have learned." He was right and it was a practice we continued. In those days there were many people to talk to.

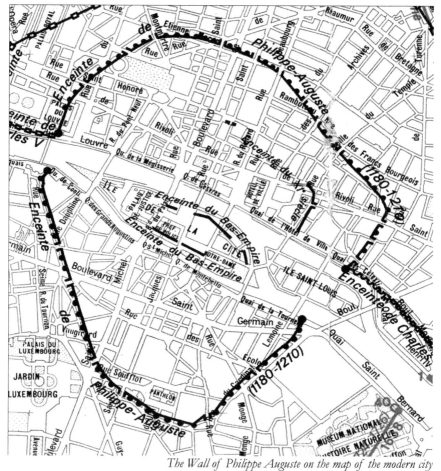

The Wall of Philippe Auguste on the map of the modern city

Another time he said to me, "Look, let's speak in English. I know you are trying to speak better French and we all appreciate this fact, but it is boring to talk with someone who can only speak French in the present tense. Have you no past or future?" Once we had a conversation at length on the differences of situation when one in English says "well" or "well, well" or "well, well, well."

My French friends called me Stoo, taking liberty and fraternity with my name.

When I would enter the bar, "Allo," Celina would say, and like in the movies we kissed once on each cheek. It was not long before I would kiss and be kissed by all the patrons. Frequently, I sat with Antoinette who made sure I understood what was being said around me, so I was not a complete fool. Sometimes I got her to sing a French song I had heard and then translate it. My favorite was Félice Aussi written and sung by the horse-faced actor and cabaret singer Fernand Joseph Désiré Contandin who called himself Fernandel in the French tradition of taking on a single appellation. In the song, a fellow in the Bois du Boulogne picks up a young girl from Burgundy named Félicie and takes her to dine at Bouillon Chartier, a workingman's restaurant. He remarks that the lobster had hair on its legs and Félicie aussi. It's one of those songs that all French people used to know.

The Night Box was cramped and people standing behind those on the coveted barstools blocked the way to the two back rooms that contained tables and chairs and ultimately the bathrooms. Roger's office was seldom used. He was a great front man for the bar when his charisma was in full cry but a poor business manager. The back room had a long banquette where he would sometimes sleep with the "orgy girls," as he called them, who stayed after closing. A bar owner with charisma in Paris does not have to sleep alone.

Having a friend who ran such a place around the corner from where I lived was a great advantage. It became my living room and where friends left messages. It was my QG, my "quarters general." It never hurt when Roger or Celina introduced me as, "the American poet." Later, when Ealy the painter managed the bar for Roger, he told a girl proximate to me, "My friend here's a poet, he wants to write down your name."

One night when Celina was off in the countryside at a weekend rave concert with her pierced and tattooed friends, Roger was in a bad state and would not rise from his place at the bar to serve his clients, mostly tourists that night led to the Night Box by a favorable review in a travel guide that deemed it one of the coolest dive bars in Paris. While Roger sunk into a dazed state, I put on an apron and waited the tables and made the drinks and played the music. This might have been my favorite night ever in Paris. I pocketed the *pour boire*, the small change tips given me.

Roger's unpredictability thrilled me. In this he reminded me of my father who was always up for a little mischief. He started trouble in bars and caves I could never find again in daylight. Everyone in the quarter knew Roger and everyone who knew him feared what he might do next. Roger was not actually dangerous, but nose to nose he would go at it with a customer he would take a sudden dislike towards.

"Fait pas chier," he would say, truncated syntax for "make no shit."

Celina would say then, "tell him something, Stoo. He listens to you."

But I knew Roger in one of his moods would listen to no one. If I was around when he made trouble with people, I stood beside him. He was my friend, and if he wanted to throw the clients out of his bar, it was up to him. I enjoyed every second of it. The nights passed amusingly in the Night Box, and when I returned to North Carolina, I missed the activity. Sitting around the Friendly Frogs Swim Club, I tried to have a pleasant demeanor. But I was tormented by the thoughts of what my Paris friends were doing, my certain knowledge that a party was going on at the Night Box without me. I could see them drinking and laughing and sometimes singing out loud to whatever music Roger was playing in the bar. There would be flirting going on, too, and I missed that.

My wife then said she was married to a teenager and I swiftly parried, "I guess that's an improvement because since the time I have known you, you've said I act like a four-year-old."

I rolled my eyes and thought of packing.

By the time I got back to Paris, Roger had gotten himself in real trouble. Celina had quit, too. Without her the bar was unmanageable. Roger was a good but slow bartender. He gave his friends drinks. He couldn't keep track of the tabs and some nights my tab was ridiculously low and others painfully high, depending on his financial needs. Courtly with women, he was taken advantage of by opportunists, a Russian prostitute in particular who cooled her heels in the Night Box when not servicing the posh hotel down the street. He would make some costly personal mistakes and depart Paris awhile, leaving Ealy in charge.

Ealy made things smoother. He brought in a professional bartender who could handle the crowd in the then-busy bar. Here in an ambience of music and laughter, I spent many nights after walking the Walls of Paris, reflecting on what it was I had seen and heard and felt. When I told my new friends what it was I had done that day, how for instance I had seen a foundation wall of the Roman Forum located on the boulevard St-Michel near the trajectory of the wall, they seemed genuinely excited both for me and my little adventures. I found this largely to be the case with the Parisians I encountered, who despite alienation from their government, expressed pride at their city and its history. Or maybe they just humored a crazy person who rambled their city searching out piles of stones.

Near number 19, quai de Conti, a plaque commemorates the spot where the Tour de Nesle stood some eighty feet high with an adjoining tower even taller. Along with a length of the Wall of Philippe Auguste, both were razed in 1665 to build the Institut de France. Beside me, two workers from a nearby construction site, curious to learn what I was doing so intensely, read along with me. The historical marker did not mention the orgies and murders by the fun-loving daughters of Philippe IV that took place in the early fourteenth century in the sundry chambers of the tower.

Compared with the construction completed on the Right Bank, Philippe Auguste's Wall on the Left Bank was hastily built. Eager to depart for the Holy Land and the next crusade, the king rushed the work. Some sections actually consisted of two thin walls with dirt and stones sandwiched between the larger stones cut at the site rather than at the Charenton quarry. The walls on the Left Bank were not as crucial. Rather than protecting the bourgeoning bourgeoisie on the Right Bank, these walls enclosed farms and scattered neighborhoods outside the Latin Quarter. In their map of 1552, the cartographers Trouchet and Hoyau drew fields and farms and vineyards still enclosed within the ramparts. The abbeys had already fortified themselves outside the boundaries of the city. If imperfectly constructed, the Left Bank Walls were also the product of their having been

Hendrik Mommers (1623-1693) View of the Tour de Nesle, the Pont Neuf, and the Ile de la Cite

paid for from Philippe Auguste's own treasury rather than the manner he raised funds on the Right Bank from donations from the merchants and the expulsion of the Jews and the confiscation of their properties.

Once the center of life in ancient Paris, the slower pace of development of the Left Bank has left more locations of the wall visible to the public than on the Right Bank where the city expanded during the Middle Ages and Early Modern period. When a century and a half later Charles V ordered the wall to be expanded on the Right Bank, it was only necessary to fortify it on the Left Bank and dig moats rather than incorporate populous new districts.

The path of the Wall of Philippe Auguste runs south-southeast from the Institut de France to the boulevard St-Michel, then east-southeast until just before the place de la Contrescarpe, and ultimately north on the rue du Cardinal Lemoine until the river where it ends on the quai de Tournelle. It is easy to see how it shaped this part of the city. Streets such as the rue Mazarine, the rue M. le Prince, the rue des Fossés St-Jacques, and the rue du Cardinal Lemoine run *extra muros*, right outside the wall. All along this

Detail of map of 1552, showing farms and fields still within the wall

route, particularly in the first section east of the rue Mazarine and the last part west of the rue du Cardinal Lemoine, the wall is integrated into the remaining buildings, and several towers are visible when one looks diligently.

On this day when I walked along the quai de Conti, the autumn light was sharp. I passed the Hotel de la Monnaie and took a left down the rue Guénégaud to numbers 27-29. The courtyard was open to several businesses that required active foot passage. To the left, outside a mailroom for one of them, I waited a few moments to see if any of employees came out into the courtyard. As was the situation at the Louvre, it is easy to strike up a conversation with someone who goes outside to smoke—not like disturbing people at their work or lunch. A clerk stepped out, lit up, and after an interlude in which he took a deep drag, I asked him if he knew about the Wall of Philippe Auguste and the base of the tower inside. He knew exactly what I was talking about. When he finished his cigarette, he welcomed me inside, gave a glance to his colleagues who nodded back, knowing what it was I was looking for, and with the exaggerated flourish of a showman, he moved a pile of cartons and presented to me the wall and adjacent tower. They appeared in good condition and fit in well with the warehouse atmosphere. Even though the tower had been obscured, I could see the employees were proud of it being in the midst of their premises.

Back down rue Guénégaud, I quickly took a right along the quai and made another quick right down under the archway of the rue de Nevers, and I took off my sunglasses because the very narrow street was dark. It was silent too, and with each step, I moved back in time. Towards the end of the street where the rue de Nesle enters it, the rue de Nevers becomes the impasse de Nevers, a blind alley. The Wall of Philippe Auguste is the reason it dead-ends here because this is the other side of the wall I saw in the mailroom on the rue Guénégaud. Workmen renovating the building next door had left scaffolding and supplies against it. The mood was shattered. Another time, the wall would be the canvas for graffiti.

I turned and went down the rue de Nesle to the rue Dauphine where amazingly a bus threaded its way through the traffic. I don't know how it is possible the drivers do this without clipping buildings, lampposts, or cars. I walked right on the rue Dauphine and headed toward the passage Dauphine. Slightly out of alignment with the passage, the rue Christine, famous in the poem by Guillaume Apollinaire "Monday rue Christine," was blocked by an amazing truck with hydraulic equipment lifting pallets of tile up to a third-floor apartment.

The passage Dauphine cuts through to the rue Mazarine, a very convenient short cut between the streets, and several businesses are located there, including the language school at number 13. When I inquired at the desk, a very kind receptionist walked me to the Philippe Auguste Lecture Hall further inside the building. She requested I turn the lights off when I was finished. There was a piano on the stage next to the chalk-colored tower.

I paused awhile and sat on the bench. My error in thinking had been that I would be able to walk straight inside or outside the wall when of course its vestiges can mostly be approached by the zig and zag of wherever they can be seen. The wall may have been built in an orderly manner, but the city around it grew less so. My beloved is made of stone, a craggy old girl who hides from me, then shows a tower here, the length of a wall there then disappears into others' houses, shops, courtyards, is thought missing, destroyed, only to appear again enough to keep my hopes up. The French can be very tolerant of those in love, if not outright celebratory. I kept following.

I turned off the lights as mademoiselle had instructed, left the language school, turned left in the passageway, and out onto the rue Mazarine, where the great poet Robert Desnos lived at number 19 before he was arrested by the Gestapo and interned in the concentration camps where he died.

impasse de Nevers, another occasion

The parking garage up the street has a tower and about forty yards of wall inside it. Once, while walking the wall with my friend the Paris historian Arthur Gillette, he darted into a doorway at 27, rue Mazarine, and with the boundless energy of an urban ibex, led me down to the base of the tower beside the parked cars. There it was with a Citroën in front of it. I could not help but marvel at it down there in the garage. I went down the stairs again for another long look then surfaced back on the rue Mazarine and continued up to the intersection of rue St-André des Arts and the corner where the Café le Buci commemorates the once nearby Buci Gate on the corner of rue André Mazet.

I crossed the street, went a few steps, and entered la Cour du Commerce St-André, a passageway that cuts from the rue St-André des Arts to boulevard St-Germain. Like many of the streets along the Left Bank of the wall, it follows the location of the moat Charles V ordered outside the walls in the 1350s. Through the window at number 4, I saw the tower rising through the center of the otherwise modern offices of the Catalonian Tourist Bureau then at that address. I went inside and paced around and smiled and climbed a staircase to see another floor where it was painted and stuccoed. People paid no attention to it. They looked at the brochures of moody Catalan landscapes and waited their turns. In the nineteenth century it had been a blacksmith

Philippe Auguste Wall in Public Parking Garage, 27, rue Mazarine

shop, and the clever smithy located his forge at the base of the tower.

Around the corner in the courtyard of the Cour de Rohan (Rouen), an apartment was built inside the top of the tower I had viewed from the other side in the Catalonian tourist bureau (now a restaurant). In the nineteenth century this tower and a ruin of ivy-covered wall was used as the terrace for a girl's school then located in the adjoining building. The painter Edouard Fournier remarked, "It is a joyful sight, to see children of the present day leaping and bounding on this remnant of antiquity."

Back in the Cour St-André, I stood outside the back entrance to Procope, one of the first cafés of Paris, where the king and god were dis-invented by free thinkers animated with coffee, while the royal spies eavesdropped from nearby tables. I continued through the passage out to boulevard St-Germain and crossed the pulsing artery. Near Odéon I looked for the rue de l'Écoles de Médecine and turned right onto the rue Antoine Dubois where two houses meet at an odd angle that follows the wall rather than the street line. This was the coach entry at numbers 2-4.

I then climbed the stairs at the end of the street and turned left onto the rue M. Prince, once called rue des Fossés M. Prince, another of the many streets named for the location along the moats that Charles V added

to enhance the fortifications on the Left Bank. Other streets: rue Fossés St-Jacques and rue Fossés St-Bernard bear these names into the twenty-first century. You can see the elevation of the street where the Crémerie Polidor restaurant has been in business since 1845.

Vestiges of the wall hide behind it and the buildings along the north side of the block running from the numbers in the forties and fifties. I tried every porte in an attempt to gain access to the courtyards, but I had no luck.

At number 45 a Chinese restaurant—La Grande Muraille, the Great Wall—was closed after lunch and the door locked. I gave it a knock and a man opened the door and stepped out into the street. I asked him if he could let me

in the courtyard adjacent to the restaurant. He took me inside and showed me he had no access to the courtyard even through the kitchen. I asked him if he knew his restaurant was situated against the wall.

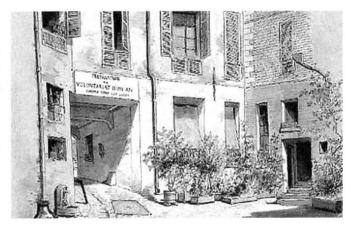

He said that he came from Hong Kong, the restaurant belonged to his cousin, and that he had never heard of Philippe Auguste.

I insisted the name of his restaurant was a good joke. He agreed and laughed agreeably.

Further up the block, I went inside an antiquarian bookstore. Three antique bespectacled bibliophiles looked up from the tomes they were lovingly appraising and gave me puzzled, but sympathetic expressions. I convinced the man to open the digicode of the courtyard next door. I saw no vestiges there. I exited the courtyard and continued along the rue M. Prince past the Luxembourg Cinema and crossed to the right side of the street where the downhill climb gave me the sense of how high the moat had been filled in, then down some seven stairs where the rue M. Prince meets the boulevard St-Michel. I crossed the heavy traffic and stopped at number 53 where Porte St-Michel once stood near where I had seen the wall of the Roman Forum beneath street level. A few blocks further

down the rue Soufflot, two towers of the Porte St-Jacques and a section of the Wall of Philippe Auguste remained well into the nineteenth century when they were destroyed during the reconstruction of the street in 1849.

The rue St-Jacques was once the Roman *cardo*, the major south-north thoroughfare, essentially the main street of ancient Paris. It was also the beginning to the Paris pilgrimage route to Campostella. Many pilgrims fortified themselves before departing, so I thought mid-way through my journey a cold beer might be in order. An unpromising brasserie a little way down the rue St-Jacques advertised new ownership in its window. I have a talent for finding such rank places and a need to enter them. No one was inside except the bartender who was perhaps also the new management and a fellow making gasping noises behind the bar. When a big hand put a wrench upon the zinc, I realized at once that he was not performing a sexual act but was, in fact, a plumber. He looked guilty nonetheless. Perhaps he knew the poor quality of his work. I drank the worst beer I ever had in Paris. It tasted watery despite or perhaps because of the plumbing problems the place was having. The plumber asked the bartender for a *fil de fer*, a hanger wire. He went about trying to clear a pipe, grunting with exertion. When I entered the toilets downstairs, I had to pee in the dark because the bulb would not illuminate, and I was careful not to slip into the Turkish toilet and enter the Porte des Égouts. Of course, no water flowed from the sink when I tried to wash my hands, and I noticed the telephone was out of order. I wondered what the previous ownership might have been like if these people felt compelled to advertise the change in management.

Just beyond the Porte St-Jacques, the angle of the wall can be seen in the row of buildings on the right side of rue Soufflot heading east toward the Pantheon. I went up the rue St-Jacques, and then left on the Fossés St-Jacques, then past the handsome town hall of the Fifth Arrondissement and the Place de l'Estrapade. I stopped at the pretty fountain where Fosses St-Jacques touches the Place de l'Estrapade and sat on a bench near the Café de la Nouveau Mairie. Nearby, a man took photos of his daughter standing by the fountain, while another daughter idled with her mother off to the side. He took many photos. She mugged for the camera; there was love in the father's lens. Perhaps she attended school at the Sorbonne a few blocks away. Or maybe she took a job in the city enacting the classic French novel outline of the young person from the countryside coming to Paris.

Looking left down the rue d'Ulm, I could see the south face of the Pantheon. Nearby, down the rue Descartes stands the church of St Etienne du Mont, one of the oldest in Paris. It was most certainly built on the site of a temple when Mont Locotecia, this neighborhood, was a Roman enclave. At the corner of rue de l'Estrapede and the rue d'Ulm where once the Porte Papale stood, the seldom-used gate the Pope entered when coming up from Italy. The porte led into the abbey of St-Genevieve and the church of St-Etienne du Mont. Nearby, in the rue Thouin, a public swimming pool is close to the Wall, and beyond it at number 16 there is a stretch of wall as well as quite a chunk inside the adjacent Lycée Henri IV. Constructed upon the filled in moat, the rue Thouin was opened in 1685. I stopped for a moment down the street at number 12 where a young couple renovated an old structure into a restaurant. I peeked inside and the back wall looked old enough to be the Wall. A young woman came out and gave me a card and promised the restaurant would open next week. From the appearance of the work left to be done, it seemed unlikely. I wished them well. I returned to sample their Provençal cuisine a few years later, but they were gone and a pizza place had opened there. At number 10, I peeked through the grating of the porte and saw the wall painted white in the dim light of the courtyard.

Above a Greek restaurant at number 50, rue Descartes, a plaque indicated the location of the Porte Bordel later called Porte St-Marcel.

A Lebanese food shop did business at number 47 and next to it was a porte to a courtyard, which I read had an archer's path inside it. I waited awhile by the entrance, and as I was about to leave a man approached the doorway and pressed the digicode to the building. I engaged him.

He said that he did not know anything about the wall but that other people had come here to look around. He invited me in—as if he had a choice—because he saw I was eager and unstoppable. I followed him into the old courtyard. The building consisted of several floors of half-timbered apartments and many staircases leading to them. I followed him up a flight to the right, and from the landing I could see the top of the wall. He pointed me toward a garden area where the primary part of this archer's path is located. It was dark in the garden, but I contented myself with having gotten in and what a clever human I was for doing so. I forgot which staircase I ascended and walked down one then another. Each was locked by a grilled gate at the bottom that I had not noticed when I first came up. Usually a button opened the porte, and I pressed the several nearby but each turned on a different light. I walked back upstairs and down another flight and tried another gate. I went back to the one I thought he initially led me up. What kind of a game was this? I considered climbing down the wall of the courtyard but it was not really possible. After about twenty anxious minutes I heard footsteps that belonged to the same man who had let me in. He carried a bag of garbage. I explained the situation and he walked me down the stairs, pressed a button hidden in the shadows and let me out, the bold adventurer.

I followed the rue de l'Estrapade to the rue Thouin and right below the place de Contrescarpe named for the escarpment. On the place de Contrescarpe, the seedy bars Ernest Hemingway described with their "flyblown tariffs and warnings against public drunkenness" have long been replaced with expensive cafes. Around the corner at 39, rue Descartes was the building in which he wrote his early stories, having learned he could write about Michigan better while living in Paris. It was also the street where Ernest Hemingway resided with his former wife, Hadley Richardson. He writes affectionately of this neighborhood in the opening pages of *A Moveable Feast*, the great double love story of his passion for both a city and himself as a young man.

I walked downhill on the rue du Cardinal Lemoine where the Wall of Philippe Auguste runs behind the rows of houses to my left into whose courtyards I had previously trespassed. Some time after I had initially walked the Wall of Philippe Auguste, I learned about an arch in the wall where the Bièvre River once flowed on its way to the Seine. The stone arch had been uncovered in the 1980s when the basement of the post office at 30, rue du Cardinal Lemoine was excavated. On the first Wednesday of every month, a tour is given by a Paris historical organization. The guide led us through several locked doors and down a staircase to an underground vault where I and a handful of school teachers visiting from Lyon marveled at the spooky arch that gleamed bone white in the half dark—or seemed to me now in my memory of it. At my feet were dried out stones of the hidden river. I did not yet know that its current would, on other occasions, bring me to its source.

Geologists believe that twelve thousand years ago, the melting of the continental glaciers caused the Seine to flood its banks and overtake the bed of its tributary, la Bièvre, along the stretch that would become Paris. Previously, the Seine flowed around to the north, entering what would be today's city near the Pont d'Austerlitz, looping the elevation of Montmartre, and merging into the Bièvre near the place d'Alma. The Bievre suffered further depredations, including having its course altered for early urban projects and culminating with the burial of its last open stretch in the city. Its contact with people pretty much killed it.

Named by the Romans after the beavers that dammed and fished its waters, the little river played many roles in urban history but only briefly as a freshet. It prefigured in Gallo-Roman Paris as a natural defense to the southeast as well as a back drop for the amphitheater (the Arena of Lutece).

Courtyard 62, rue du Cardinal Lemoine

As the city expanded, the Bièvre got diverted through the Latin Quarter to provide power for mills, then split off again to irrigate the lands of the Abbey St-Victor. Due to the blood of the slaughterhouses, the dyes from the Gobelins Tapestry works, the grease of the tanneries, the toxins of the paint and gunpowder factories, and a thousand years of insults, the authorities declared it a health hazard nearly four hundred years ago, though it had been evolving into one for centuries. Its smell was well-known and repugnant. Rue Mouffetard derives from the *mouffes*, the malodorous expressions of the slow moving current. As Paris developed, the river was partially covered, and by the 1950s, its entire urban course had disappeared. It now enters the sewer system and plays an important role in the diversion of storm water. You can follow the streets above it and imagine how it would appear flowing through the Jardins des Plantes or the Square Rene Le Gall, or you can walk along its banks in segments to Guyancourt as I have done.

Down the block I went inside the courtyard at number 62 where a section can be seen encased as a boundary wall through this block of houses. By my calculations this would be the other side of the wall I saw inside 47, rue Descartes where I was temporarily imprisoned. Here the wall sealed off the back of the courtyard. Flowerboxes formed a pediment in front of it and ivy crept between the stones. Someone had leaned a tire against it.

Around the corner on the rue Clovis (5-7), a jagged piece of the wall like a stale slice of precious cake, extends into the sidewalk similar to the vestige across the river on the rue Charlemagne. I could put my arms around it. I did, then jaywalked across rue Clovis in the busy afternoon traffic, climbed on the handrailing across the street, and saw how deeply the path of the wall ran back through the block. I also noticed what a high spot this was with a view across the river perhaps as far as Bagnolet to the Northeast. I crossed back over and walked down Clovis to number 7 that has a modern looking grillwork that prevents entrance to the building. A woman about to walk her small terrier

rue Clovis

approached. I explained my mission to her, and she generously let me in the porte.

Deep in the courtyard, she showed me the expanse of the wall and its archer's path. She pulled back her arm to indicate the archer. We both laughed. She seemed genuinely excited I expressed interest in this. She told me where more of the wall can be seen at the fire station around the block. I called her, "très gentille" which she was. She told me I spoke French well, which I did not.

Another, shorter length of the wall was spared when the city constructed the firehouse at 68, rue du Cardinal Lemoine and rue J.-H. Lartigue. It is a modern station, and the firemen seemed friendly. I continued to 9, rue d'Arras which in other days was named rue des Murs, the street of the Wall. This area used to be all vineyards, dating back to Gallo-Roman times. Additionally, I have tried my luck at numbers 9-11 and the door was always locked. I wondered what hid back there and what of the Wall remains after the renovation of this modern-looking façade. In France one never knows what is waiting

Porte St-Victor and the Chateau de Tournelle

behind a porte or wall. Sometimes wealth and sometimes squalor.

At 7, rue des Chantiers, now a Masonic temple, a plaque indicated a part of wall was discovered here during construction work in 1878. Across the street a trace can be observed cracking through the plasterwork of the façade at number 4. At 7, boulevard St-Germaine, a skinny building, is sandwiched in the width of the wall located between the two apartment houses similar to the structure I had seen on the rue St-Honoré.

The Left Bank wall ended at 3, quai de la Tournelle where the round defense tower, la Tournelle, had been built by Philippe Auguste to guard the easternmost edge of the city as the Tour de Nesle had been erected to the west. It was taken down a couple of hundred years later and replaced with the Chateau de la Tournelle, a fort consisting of square turrets. It was repurposed as a prison and destroyed during the Revolution. One of the most expnsive restuarants in the world, le Tour d'Argent, occupies the site.

During the reign of Louis XIV, Blondel constructed a ceremonial gate here also—the Porte St-Bernard—similar to the ones he built at Porte St-Denis and Porte St-Martin. I felt tired from walking, but nonetheless imagined walking triumphantly through it.

Stuart Dischell was born in Atlantic City, NJ. He is the author of Good Hope Road, *a National Poetry Series Selection,* Evenings & Avenues, Dig Safe, Backwards Days *and* Children With Enemies *and the pamphlets* Animate Earth *and* Touch Monkey, *along with the chapbook* Standing on Z. *His poems have appeared in* The Atlantic, Agni, The New Republic, Slate, Kenyon Review, Ploughshares, *and anthologies including* Essential Poems, Hammer and Blaze, Pushcart Prize, *and Garrison Keillor's* Good Poems. *A recipient of awards from the NEA, the North Carolina Arts Council, and the John Simon Guggenheim Foundation, he teaches in the MFA Program in Creative Writing at the University of North Carolina Greensboro.*

Tyehimba Jess

Pre/face
Berryman/Brown

The poem then,	Let me say,
whatever its wide cast of characters,	despite loss…I won my life. This story—
is essentially about	how a slave steals back his skin:
an imaginary character	smuggles loose like I did. It lives on,
(not the poet,	but through words—and
not me)	free. I'm
named Henry,	"Box" Brown. Ain't
a white American	masking my truth: one day,
in early middle age,	I delivered myself.
sometimes	I ache
in	my
blackface,	love for
who has suffered	…those left behind.
an irreversible loss	…Berryman can't talk for them,
and talks about himself…	can't tell my tale at all.

Italicized text excerpted from John Berryman's introductory note to
The Dream Songs.

Reprinted from *Olio* by permission of the author.

Freedsong: Dream Dawn

Thus passed my child from my presence...I could only say, farewell, and leave it to pass in its chains while I looked for the approach of another gang in which my wife was also loaded with chains.
—*Narrative of the Life of Henry Box Brown*

There sat down, hard, a thing upon Henry's heart
so heavy, if he had a hundred years
& more, & weeping, sleepless, in all that time
Henry would not make good.
Starts again always in Henry's fears
a brittle loss somewhere. His old love, his wife.

And there is a smothered thing he has in mind—
like a grave comedy's fate. A thousand years
would fail to blur her still profile in the dusk. Ghastly,
with closed eyes, he pretends she's nigh.
All his cells say: too late. Then there are his tears,
sinking.

But never did Henry, as some thought he should,
end a master and hack their body up
and hide the pieces where they wouldn't be found.
He knows he wanted to. So, he went gone. He went missing.
Often he reckons, on the dawn, his love.
Her body is ever missing.

From "Dream Song 29"

Reprinted from *Olio* by permission of the author.

Sissieretta Jones, Carnegie Hall, 1902:

O patria mia.

Aida, buried in the darkness
of her fate. Aida, singing
in the tomb of her lover.
Her lover a notion pale as
the aria circling from her mouth.
Aida, lowered into the pit
cloaked in breath's ocean,
 a war inside her voice.
A battle of tongues sung *doloroso*,
the husk of shadow on air.
With the soar of her father's
sermon for truth. With the burn
of nigger heaven. With the hum
of oceans wrapped in bone.
With the legacy of bones
wrapped in ocean. With a national
healing hogtied to song.
Let me hum it to you sweet
with *vivace*; let me scrape it into
our history. Let my voice turn
its scarred back on you.
Let my skin disappear
to cover you whole.
Let my molten song be
your blessing of ash.
Let the ash cover all
our faces. Let ash be

the secret that masters
itself. Let the curtain rise
upon the hidden face.
Let the spotlight burn
to purify need. Nail down
the lockbox of spirituals
inside my throat. Bury
them in opera's echo
of grandeur. Resurrect the holy
grind of *tremolo* and tradition.
Let the key be infinite.
Let the coon song scatter.
Let each mouth be envy.
Let bloodlines be muddied.
I stand solo in this country
of concert. I am multitudes
of broken chains. I am Aida
with war on her lips.
I am Aida against drowning
in all that summons her alive.
I bear the crescendo
of ocean inside me.
I carry its bones inside
my attack. I am a wave
reaching beyond this shore.
Let this belting be our
unbinding. Let *o* bring
the sound of all our wanting.
Let *patria* speak the names
of all my fathers.
Let the curtain rise
to show the face that is
known. Let the country
be mine. Let the country
be mine. Let this country
be mine.

Reprinted from *Olio* by permission of the author.

My Name Is Sissieretta Jones

Once word got out about the way I sing, the world wanted to bleed all the sass out my name. To scratch out the gift my mother gave me and shove a would-be white diva in my spotlight. They couldn't imagine the colored in *coloratura* just standing on its own on stage, so they claimed I was just part of Adelina Patti's chorus. They stuck me beneath her name, a shadow sentenced to the borders of her light, called me Black Patti.

But the darkened sense inside my name won't be silenced. With its *sister* and *shush* and gospel of ocean, I sing each night from the way I'd stand on the docks of Providence, a straggle-boned bundle of lungs and tremble lifting wave after wave into wave after wave of Atlantic. Its applause keeled over me, calling me with its bell of salt, its belly of sunken hulls, its blue green fathoms of tremolo. Every night, in the dark offstage, I hear my mother's voice in my head, her backyard hum, the sea in her distance with the weather of storm. She'd look out and see the thrall of water heave its back to the sky. I'd look out to the darkness and hear my true name.

Tyehimba Jess is the author of two books of poetry, Leadbelly *and* Olio. Olio *won the 2017 Pulitzer Prize, the Anisfield-Wolf Book Award, The Midland Society Author's Award in Poetry, and received an Outstanding Contribution to Publishing Citation from the Black Caucus of the American Library Association. It was also nominated for the National Book Critics Circle Award, the PEN Jean Stein Book Award, and the Kingsley Tufts Poetry Award.* Leadbelly *was a winner of the 2004 National Poetry Series. The Library Journal and Black Issues Book Review both named it one of the "Best Poetry Books of 2005."*

Reprinted from *Olio* by permission of the author.

Tarfia Faizullah

The First Lesson

If the thin mist from rain
must reckon with the pulsing
of stars radiant in their dying,

then I too must first admit
that I don't know
before I can believe.

The way I believe the earth
I live on is an orb. You tremble,
and I try to soften the fist

of your fear with a hand
that sought solace once
in the symmetry of a golfball

when the hand that raised me
was raised. I knew
I deserved it, but I believe

what you taught me: that I also
deserve to lavish the sun
on my wrists when they feel too

delicate. If the train trembling past
our house is a vibration I feel
amplifying my spine as it shudders

into place against yours, then I must
be willing to believe I am free.
Free, the way Muhammad

believed: to read without knowing
he knew how to read. I mean, I don't
know—did I or didn't I dream the world

out of a drop of saliva from the mouth
of a thirsty god? Does an astronomer
ever feel like a fraud? I've been trying

to pretend like I knew all along.
I've been trying to dream the world
in which the memory of any hurt

I ever caused you didn't
exist. Instead, they are the slender
shivers of light rippling across

an open register of unmarked
graves. Instead, they are the songs
an orphan sings when she's no longer

afraid. We dream this world
without a plan. Without sight.
It's only when we wake that we

believe again the first lesson:
no one wants to learn how to fight.

What I Want Unlocks Itself

At the Halloween party
the vampire congratulates me
on my corset as though
I've been promoted

or had a child. It prickles
like coldwater dawns I loved

turning a coin and the sky
between my fingers.

A zombie knocks past
the punch bowl. Don't
flinch. Put your arm

around him. It's easy
to thistle the air
into fortune with a lit cigarette,

harder to lean into the werewolf
who begs me to unzip him.

In the drawer I never left
open at home are the blades
of scissors pressed together
like the thighs of the drunk dinosaur

passed out across the stairs,
the one who reached past me

into the bowl of eyeballs
and laughed, I mean,

if you can't fuck
in paradise, where can you? It's easy

to not think about how my father
might feel if he saw how I snip

gardens of plums out of my clothes
and lacerate my inner thighs.

An astronaut cups my ass as we dance.
The drunk dinosaur wakes, whimpers
because she couldn't rawr
that she never wanted it,
that the spikes on her tail

were always naturally
golden. What I want locks itself
into the same old muzzle, passes again
into the mosque

on Midland Drive beside
Mrs. Baird's. It was there I first
learned the word

shame could rise
with a shape and a scent and a taste.

Denial

If you deny that you are a muscle
encrusted with skull, easily
punctured through skin—small,
a stringed instrument
to play or prop against a wall—
then in between her kisses,
you must also deny

that you slough your morals
from the wreckage of silt
caught low in another woman's
bones.
        Sometimes you unpeel
each bruise from the child
you were, a universe confined
in glass, and sometimes it's not
the right fit, that blazer that cinches
your waist

        into a stem anyone wants
to cuff, and sometimes, you can see
that you are a skeleton so many
fingers have felt up against
the rotting bricks of sky-rinsed
alleys.
        If you deny that you
are worthy of love, then
denial will still be the sound
the inside of your wrist

makes as you hold a lit match
to it, knowing that neither parent
nor priest, neither shotgun
nor her lips dusted with sugar
can ever stop you.

Tarfia Faizullah was born in 1980 in Brooklyn, New York, and raised in Midland, Texas. She is the author of a previous poetry collection, Seam, *winner of a VIDA Award, a GLCA New Writers' Award, a Milton Kessler First Book Award, Drake University Emerging Writer Award, and other honors. Her poems are published widely in periodicals and anthologies both in the United States and abroad, are translated into Persian, Chinese, Bengali, Tamil, and Spanish, have been featured at the Smithsonian, the Rubin Museum of Art, and elsewhere, and are the recipients of multiple awards, including three Pushcart Prizes, the Frederick Bock Prize from Poetry, and others. In 2016, she was recognized by Harvard Law School's Women Inspiring Change. Faizullah currently teaches in the University of Michigan Helen Zell Writers' Program as the Nicholas Delbanco Visiting Professor in Poetry.*

Robin Fulton Macpherson

Life in the Universe

If only the trees would stop rushing past,
stay where they are
so that from a still point I could watch them.

We grow weary balancing on the edge
of ellipses.

Nasturtium Nightmare

I planted small ones, got big ones:
leaves as wide as wide umbrellas
blocked out my southern horizon
then darkened the highest heavens
with an unfathomable green.
Blossoms shrank to ochre pinpoints.
The pinpoints shrank into the night.
Watching them I too was a point
perhaps some day detectable
in a fuzz of radio waves.

In the 1960s and 1970s Robin Fulton Macpherson was active in Scottish literary life as a poet, reviewer and editor. Since 1973 his home base has been in Norway and in the decades since he has built a solid reputation as a translator of Scandinavian poets, such as Tomas Tranströmer, Kjell Espmark and Harry Martinson from Swedish and Olav H. Hauge from Norwegian. His A Northern Habitat: Collected Poems 1960-2010 *was published by Marick Press in 2013.*

Thomas Lux

It's the Little Towns I Like

It's the little towns I like,
with their little mills making ratchets
and stanchions, elastic web,
spindles, you
name it. I like them in New England,
America, particularly—providing
bad jobs good enough to live on, to live in
families even: kindergarten,
church suppers, beach umbrellas....The towns
are real, so fragile in their loneliness
a flood could come along
(and floods have) and cut them in two,
in half. There is no mayor,
the town council's not prepared
for this, three of the four policemen
are stranded on their roofs...and it doesn't stop
raining. The mountain
is so thick with water, parts of it just slide
down on the heifers—soggy, suicidal—
in the pastures below. It rains, it rains
in these towns and, because
there's no other way, your father gets in a rowboat
so he can go to work.

Reprinted from *New and Selected Poems: 1975-1995* by permission.

Elegy for Frank Stanford

1949-1978

A message from the secretary tells me first
the heavy clock you were
in your mother's lap
has stopped. Later, I learned who
stopped it: you,
with three lead thuds,
determined insults, to your heart.
You dumb fuck, Frank.
I assume, that night, the seminarians
were mostly on their knees
and on their dinner plates only a few
wing bones—quiet flutes
ahead of the wind....I can almost
understand, Frank: your nerves'
oddometer needle waving
in *danger*, your whole
body, in fact, ping-raked, a rainbow
disassembling. You woke, in the dark,
dreaming a necklace of bloodsuckers....
But that final gesture,
Frank: irreversible cliché!
The long doorman of the east continues
his daily job, bending slightly
at the waist to wave dawn past.
Then the sparrows begin
their standard tunes, every day, Frank,
every day. There's the good hammer-
music in the poles
of north and south; there's the important

rasp of snake over desert and rock;
there's agriculture—even when it fails:
needle-sized carrots, blue pumpkins;
and presidencies, like yours, Frank,
of dredging companies, but presidencies....
You must have been desiring exit badly.
So now, you're a bit of gold to pound
back into the earth, the dew, of course,
forever lapping your toes, —
Frank, you dumb fuck, —who loves you
loves you regardless.

Reprinted from *New and Selected Poems: 1975-1995* by permission.

Motel Seedy

The artisans of this room, who designed the lamp base
(a huge red slug with a hole
where its heart should be) or chose this print
of a butterscotch sunset,
must have been abused in art class
as children, forced to fingerpaint
with a nose, or a tongue. To put this color
green—exhausted grave grass—to cinder blocks
takes an understanding of loneliness
and/or institutions that terrifies.
It would seem not smart to create
a color scheme in a motel room
that's likely to cause impotence in men
and open sores in women,
but that's what this puce bedspread
with its warty, ratty tufts could do. It complements
the towels, torn and holding awful secrets
like the sail on a life raft
loaded with blackened, half-eaten corpses…
I think I owned this desk once, I think
this chair is where I sat
with the Help Wanted ads spread and wobbling
before me as I looked for jobs
to lead me upward: to rooms
like this, in America, where I dreamed
I lived…Do I deprive tonight
the beautician and her lover,
a shower-head salesman, of this room?
He is so seldom in town.

I felt by their glance in the hallway
that my room, no. 17, means
something (don't ask me to explain this) special
to them. Maybe they fell fiercely
into each other here for the first time,
maybe there was a passion preternatural. I'm glad
this room, so ugly, has known some love
at $19.00 double occupancy—
though not tonight, for a dollar fifty less.

Reprinted from *The Drowned River* by permission.

"Mr. John Keats Five Feet Tall" Sails Away

on the *Maria Crowther*,
a cargo brig
of 127 tons bound for Italy,
Naples, the sun
which was thought would cure his cough, his lungs.
The day: Sunday, 17 September 1820.
With him: Severn,
a painter, his nurse-companion;
Mrs. Pidgeon, a pain in the ass
and cold; Miss Cotterell,
like Keats consumptive
and "very lady-like but a sad martyr
to her illness," wrote Severn;
the captain and crew.
This was not a pleasure cruise.
Second day out: the sick
and nonsick get seasick
and "bequeath to the mighty sea their breakfasts."
Storms, water by the pailful
in the sleeping cabin; calms, nary a puff.
A squall (Bay of Biscay),
a calm again (Cape Saint Vincent),
then, one dawn, Gibraltar, the African coast!
Then, Bay of Naples,
Saturday, 21 October—ten days
quarantined
during which not one porthole opened
it rained so hard and long.
Welcome, Mr. Keats, to sunny southern Italy.

Then, by wagon, on roads ripe
with malaria, to Rome
from where in the two months plus
he still has lungs
he does not write again to Fanny Brawne,
whom he loves,
though he does write about
her to a friend
the famous sentence: "Oh God! God! God!" (in whom
he had no faith) "Every thing
I have in my trunk
reminds me of her
and goes through me like a spear."
And the better but less quoted
next sentence: "The silk
lining she put in my travelling cap scalds
my head." The verb choice "scalds"
perfect here (literally he had the fever,
figuratively…), the tactility
fresher, the melodrama cut
by an almost comic hyperbole. It is
more Keats than Keats,
who died 172 years, 8 months, 2 weeks, and 4 days
ago—this tiny man
John Keats,
who wrote some poems
without which,
inch by inch—in broken
barn light,
in classrooms (even there!),
under the lamp where what you read
teaches you what you love—without which
we could each,
inch by hammered inch,
we would each
be diminished.

Reprinted from *New and Selected Poems: 1975-1995* by permission.

Thomas Lux (1946-2017) published 16 books: 15 of poetry and one of nonfiction. To the Left of Time *(poetry) was published by Houghton Mifflin Harcourt in 2016. He also edited and wrote the introduction for* I Am Flying Into Myself: Selected Poems of Bill Knott *(Farrar, Straus and Giroux, 2017). Lux taught at Sarah Lawrence College for 27 years, and then held the Margaret T. and Henry C. Bourne Chair in Poetry at the Georgia Institute of Technology (2002-2017). As director of Poetry@Tech, he brought over 150 poets to Georgia Tech to read and/or teach under Poetry@Tech's auspices. His awards included the Kingsley Tufts Prize, three grants from the NEA, a Guggenheim Fellowship, the Robert Creeley Prize, and the Georgia Governor's Award for the Humanities.*

CPSIA information can be obtained
at www.ICGtesting.com
Printed in the USA
FSOW04n1753201017
40123FS

9 780990 996156